KU-048-765

Lee Tae-Sang is a journalist, columnist, and published author of twenty-five books. This includes five translations into Korean: Kahlil Gibran's *The Prophet*, *The Garden of the Prophet*, *Spirits Rebellious*, *Nymphs of the Valley*, and Thomas Mann's *Transposed Heads*.

He has worked within the publishing industry in both Korea and England and is the founder of an online newspaper. He studied religion and philosophy and owned several businesses. As a court interpreter for the City of New York for the past 18 years, he has found the ideal place to reflect on the path of his unpredictable, global life and observe the present human condition.

To my grandchildren, Elijah, Theodore, and Julia.

Lee Tae-Sang

COSMIAN RHAPSODY

AUSTIN MACAULEY PUBLISHERS™

LONDON · CAMBRIDGE · NEW YORK · SHARJAH

Copyright © Lee Tae-Sang (2020)

All rights reserved. No part of this publication may be reproduced, distributed, or transmitted in any form or by any means, including photocopying, recording, or other electronic or mechanical methods, without the prior written permission of the publisher, except in the case of brief quotations embodied in critical reviews and certain other noncommercial uses permitted by copyright law. For permission requests, write to the publisher.

Any person who commits any unauthorized act in relation to this publication may be liable to criminal prosecution and civil claims for damages.

This is a work of creative nonfiction. The events are portrayed to the best of author's memory. While all the stories in this book are true, some names and identifying details have been changed to protect the privacy of the people involved.

Ordering Information:
Quantity sales: special discounts are available on quantity purchases by corporations, associations, and others. For details, contact the publisher at the address below.

Publisher's Cataloging-in-Publication data
Tae-Sang, Lee
Cosmian Rhapsody

ISBN 9781645752882 (Paperback)
ISBN 9781645752899 (Hardback)
ISBN 9781645752905 (ePub e-book)

Library of Congress Control Number: 2020904679

www.austinmacauley.com/us

First Published (2020)
Austin Macauley Publishers LLC
40 Wall Street, 28th Floor
New York, NY 10005
USA

mail-usa@austinmacauley.com
+1 (646) 5125767

Table of Contents

Foreword

Was the grass wet with early morning dew
to pay your dues of life and love?
Were they dewdrops of life-giving
and love-making,
or rather teardrops of joy and sorrow?
Was that for breathing in
this magic world to the full,
and breathing it out to the last,
before transforming back
into the mystical essence of the Cosmos?

Preface:
The Magic of Myth

We have an old proverb in Korea:

"Watch your words. They become seeds. What you utter, comes true."

In a tale from China, a magician gives a young peasant boy an enchanted paintbrush that brings whatever he paints to life.

Harold and the Purple Crayon, a children's picture book by Crockett Johnson, is the story of a boy exploring the world of his imagination. It's a world where whatever he draws becomes reality, a world that is only a playground for him. As for the child still alive in us, we too can become part of Harold's world, making it our favorite quote from Eleanor Roosevelt: "The future belongs to those who believe in the beauty of their dreams."

So, each and every one of us is creating one's own myth and thereby one's own life journey.

1. The Essence of Cosmos: A Thought on Soul

What is the soul? One has to wonder.

The concept of the soul may vary, from the East to the West, from a person to another.

In East Asia, it's generally understood that the soul consists of breath, which will be scattered into the sky as the dead body turns into dust.

When my father died, I was five years old. When I looked at him in the coffin, his physical appearance, alive or dead, was the same to me.

Then what's the difference between the two, I started wondering. After much thought, I concluded that as long as one keeps breathing, you're alive, and that as soon as one stops breathing, you're dead. If so, then we have to say that breath, life and soul are the same. Isn't it?

The English word "soul" is said to have come from an old German word "See," meaning the sea, based on the belief that life arises from and returns to the sea. And from about the 10th century, it's also said the word "spirit," meaning the soul of a dead person as God's breath, has come into use.

No doubt, we all are like The Little Prince of Antoine de Saint-Exupéry, who happened to land on the planet Earth as a brief sojourner and returned to his star, getting rid of his physical body with the assistance of a snake in the desert.

There are innumerable galaxies and stars, universes and multiverses in the cosmos. When all these cosmic waves rise and fall, they become the Sea of Cosmos. Wouldn't the core, the Heart of the Sea, be the very essence of us all in the Cosmos? It wouldn't matter whether it's called ghost, phantom, spirit, soul or God. Would it?

Ah—ha—that's how and why I must have composed this "little poem" as a "little prince" myself at the tender age of ten, giving myself a new name "해심" in Korean and "海心" in Chinese, meaning "the heart of the sea." I have been using it as my pen-name ever since.

The Sea

Thou symbolizing eternity
Infinity and the absolute
Art God.

How agonizing a spectacle
Is life in blindness
Tumbled into Thy callous cart
To be such a dreamy sod!

A dreamland of the gull
Of sorrow and loneliness full

Where would it be?
Beyond mortal reach would it be?
May humanity be
A sea of compassion!
My heart itself be
A sea of communion!

I envy Thy heart
Containing Passions of the sun
And Fantasies of the sky.

I long for Thy bosom
Nursing childlike enthusiasm
And All-embracing mother nature.

Although a drop of water,
It trickles into the sea.

2. *Cosmos, the Earth, and I*

"Cosmos": What an infinitely mysterious entity absolutely and utterly beyond human imagination!

"The Earth": What a stunningly and sorrowfully beautiful entity of pure mystery, a droplet of (or mist over) the Sea of Cosmos, or a grain of sand at the beach thereof!

"And I": What a breathtakingly wonderful entity of pure miracle, as a microcosmos of The Earth, the microcosmos of Cosmos, the macrocosmos!

There is "The Astronomer" from "THE MADMAN: His Parables and Poems" (1918) by Kahlil Gibran (1883-1931).

In the shadow of the temple, my friend and I saw a blind man sitting alone. And my friend said, "Behold the wisest man of our land."

Then I left my friend and approached the blind man and greeted him. And we conversed.

After a while, I said, "Forgive my question, but since when hast thou been blind?"

"From my birth," he answered.

Said I, "And what path of wisdom followest thou?"

Said he, "I am an astronomer."

Then he placed his hand upon his breast saying, "I watch all these suns and moons and stars."

3. The Aesthetics of Presence

Didn't someone say in English that "to explain is to reduce?"

There is a "sijo" (one of the traditional types of Korean poem) verse:

"With words one too many, it becomes too wordy."

In Korean, we say that it's only nagging and nitpicking to utter a word as a killjoy or a spoiler, meaning that it should go without saying, needless to say, to avoid redundancy.

In his poem "Evocation," Korean poet Kim So-Wol (1902-1934) exclaims:

Evocation

A name shattered to pieces!
A name scattered in the void!
A name that never replies!
A name that I'll die calling!

The one word left in the soul
To the last, I couldn't pronounce.
My beloved!
My beloved!

The red sun hovers over the hill,
And the deer moan woefully.
I'm calling your name
On a lonely hill.

I call your name in great sorrow.
I call your name in deep sorrow.
My voice reaches towards the sky,
But the sky is too far from the earth.

Turn me into stone,
I'll call your name till I die.
My beloved!
My beloved!

There is "The Love Song" from "THE WANDERER: His Parables and Sayings" (1932) by Kahlil Gibran (1883-1931):

The Love Song

A poet once wrote a love song and it was beautiful. And he made many copies of it, and sent them to his friends and his acquaintances, both men and women, and even to a young woman whom he had met but once, who lived beyond the mountains.

And in a day or two, a messenger came from the young woman bringing a letter. And in the letter, she said, "Let me assure you, I am deeply touched by the love song that you have written to me. Come now, and see my father and my mother, and we shall make arrangements for the betrothal."

And the poet answered the letter, and he said to her, "My friend, it was but a song of love out of a poet's heart, sung by every man to every woman."

And she wrote again to him saying, "Hypocrite and liar in words! From this day unto my coffin-day, I shall hate all poets for your sake."

Ah, that's why the American philosopher/essayist Ralph Waldo Emerson (1803-1882) must have stated:

"Use what language you will, you can never say anything but what you are."

If so, may no words be the presence!

And may love be enough unto itself!

4. "Why Am I Being Diminished When I Stand Before You?"

This is the title of Korean Singer Kim Soo-hee's hit song.

Let's apply this question to all kinds of prizes including the Nobel Prizes. Many publishers, writers, and readers are reported to have been greatly disappointed by the earlier news that there would be no Nobel Prize for Literature to be awarded in 2018.

I was prompted by this little brouhaha to think about prizes in earnest.

Whatever the presents or the prizes might be, wasn't it much more gratifying to give them than to receive them? Come to think of it, giving them out to somebody is really giving them to oneself. Isn't it?

Whoever your sweetheart is, be it your parents, siblings, friends, lovers, spouses, children, and grandchildren, if you've ever really loved someone with all your heart and soul, you'd rather bear all the burden yourself to alleviate it from your loved one whom you could never love enough.

Be that as it may, your self-worth and raison d'être is not bestowed upon yourself only when you are recommended for recognition to be presented with a prize. Does it?

As it were, no matter how great they may be, for example, all works of art are nothing more than imitations of nature and life. How could we then value the shadow more than the real thing?

Furthermore, nobody knows for sure whether there is such a thing called God or not. Even if such a divine super-being does exist indeed, nobody is sure whether it's male, female, neuter, asexual, or what. How then could anyone say this or that about such an unknown and unknowable being?

How then could one worship such an unreal phantomlike being—indoctrinated as all-knowing, almighty, all-present, all self-righteous—while failing to love and serve all things including oneself of the Cosmos from-to-in the moment?

It behooves us, then, to mind our immediate business of learning diligently as life-long students of the School of Love. Thus, enlightened altogether, we all may graduate to become Cosmians Arainbow.

5. *To Possess or to Live*

As the holiday season is upon us, there are more occasions to spend money. Of course, money is earned to be spent. But the sense of happiness one feels can vary, depending on how money is spent for what purpose, say parties, travels, gifts, etc.

A study by Harvard psychiatrist George Vaillant (b. 1943) followed 268 undergraduates from the classes of 1938-1940 for 75 years. The findings were reported in "Triumphs of Experience: The Men of the Harvard Grant Study." In the book that was first published in 2012, the Professor at Harvard Medical School and Director of Research for the Department of Psychiatry presents, based on his research studies conducted for 42 years since 1966, five lessons from the study pertaining to a happy and meaningful life.

First, the most important thing for meaning and happiness is loving relationships, without which no successful careers and good health are fulfilling.

Second, money and power have little to do with happiness. Those who feel most proud of their achievements are those who are most content in their work, not the ones who make the most money, not the ones who grab the most power.

Third, no matter how humble and poor one starts one's life, s/he can become happier and happier in life as one proceeds through it, overcoming all the adversities and hardships.

Fourth, connection with people and work is most essential for joy and happiness, increasingly more so as one ages.

Fifth and finally, how well you cope with challenges and meet them with courage and confidence will decide how happy you can be and how fulfilled you will feel.

The key to happiness and fulfillment in a nutshell—it seems to make clear—is "to replace narcissism with mature coping mechanisms like concerns for others and productive work."

Based on my own experience of living 83 years, I'd put it like this:

True happiness can be felt not from possessions but from living itself, from loving someone or something at that; neither people nor things can be possessed; you are living as much as you are caring and loving them, and consequently "you" are becoming "me," myself.

6. *You Are What You Eat*

According to the recent news reported by The Associated Press and others, 69-year-old Dutch TV personality Emile Ratelband has asked a court for a new birthday that legally would make him 49. Mr. Ratelband, a self-styled positivity guru, argued that age is just a number, and the Dutchman wants his changed.

The Arnhem District Court refused his request saying that age is nothing but a number, but it's not a number we can change as we see fit.

Since the earliest days of human history, especially in ancient India and Greece, the riddle of time must have exercised people's minds, the philosophers' in particular.

In Greek mythology, Khronos (or Chronus to the Romans) was the personification of time. The Greeks are said to have had two different words for time: Khronos and Kairos. The former refers to numeric or chronological time, while the latter refers to the more qualitative concept of the right or opportune moment.

In Korean, we say we "eat age." The implication seems to me that how and what you "eat" decides your age.

We're used to the popular saying that "you are what you eat."

Wouldn't this mean that
when you eat love, you beget love;
when you eat hatred, you beget hatred;
when you eat hope, you beget hope;
when you eat despair, you beget despair;
thus your life, or rather each breath
of yours is destined to become either
a blessing of the Cosmos or a curse of the Chaos?

7. An Open Love Letter to Ms. Jeong Yeo-Ul

Hello! I'm an 82-year-old man living in New Jersey, U.S.A. I've been enjoying reading your column articles published in Korean dailies with great admiration. I was unable to restrain my urgent impulse to take this liberty of writing to you after reading your article "Craving For A Better Life" in the "Fragrance of Life" column of The Joongang Ilbo/Korea Daily, New York Edition (December 12, 2018). You concluded your article by saying: *"Only if there are objects to love, as long as we have things to love to do, life to love, we'll be O.K. Today I feel like to embrace myself most warmly and tightly with all my might, though I'm still imperfect, insecure and sorrowful."* Wow, in this short phrase, you condensed the essence of life, all the sum, and substance of philosophy and literature. You are a prodigy and a genius, indeed! Yes, indeed, I for one totally agree with you in that as long as there are objects to love, we couldn't be happier. Wouldn't it be? All things in Nature are being objects to love, and thereby I myself become the object itself. That's why I have come to believe that one does live as much as one does love, and that loving someone or something is really loving oneself. Ever since my long-gone yesteryears when I came across these two gems that struck the tender core of my heart and soul, scarring me forever, I couldn't help chanting them as my heart beats and even beyond...

> *There is a lady sweet and kind,*
> *Was never a face so pleased my mind;*
> *I did but see her passing by,*
> *And yet I love her till I die.*

English poet Barnabe Googe
(1540-94).

Eternity consisted of a flash of a lightning-like moment when we became the very object of our love.—German mystic Jakob Boehme (1575-1624).

The poet who wrote the verse quoted above must have seen the Lady in person. Although I have not met you, and yet I feel the same. Ha—Ha—I'm dead serious. I don't know who named you, "여울(Yeo-ul)" in Korean meaning rapids/shallows. How I wish I could join you even for a moment as a fellow drop of the current in your stream flowing into the Sea of Cosmos!

Sincerely, Lee Tae-Sang
December 21, 2018
Tenafly, New Jersey, U.S.A.

8. An Open Letter to Mr. Haruki Murakami

Dear Mr. Haruki Murakami,

Today I read your interview article with Sarah Lyall of The New York Times (October 10, 2018) and I was impressed. I agree with you that "a book is a metaphor." You expressed my cherished thoughts so poetically.

I do like your statement very much: "If you close your eyes and dive into yourself, you can see a different world. It's like exploring the cosmos, but inside yourself." Wow, you were speaking for me too!

All the while, living my life for eighty-two years, I've never dreamed that there would be a day like today, one day. Looking back, had I not lost my first love almost sixty years ago, I could not have come to realize that I, and all others, all beings are "cosmians" born "arainbow" from the Cosmos. A young boy who happened to fall in love with the microcosmos of a flower ended up embracing the whole of the macrocosmos.

Your answer was: "I don't have to dream, because I can write," when you were asked at the end of the interview: "What do you dream about?" You said: "I'm a realistic person, a practical person, but when I write fiction, I go to weird, secret places in myself. What I am doing is an exploration of myself—inside myself."

In my case, I didn't have to write fiction, because I've been living my dreams, being aware from early on that facts were stranger than fiction and that life itself was but a dream. As the published author of 24 books (including 5 translations: Thomas Mann's Transposed Heads and Kahlil Gibran's The Prophet, The Garden of the Prophet, Spirits Rebellious and The Nymphs of The Valley)—all in Korean except three in English (including two now in the process of being published), all based on my own life, I couldn't agree more with Ralph Waldo Emerson when he said: "Use what language you will, you can never say anything but what you are." Ever since my earliest childhood, I aspired to write on the invisible sheet of life with the pen of living in the ink of blood, sweat, and tear of love, and I'm still striving on.

I am writing this letter, seeking your help, perchance, through your huge readership, in reaching out to find a Japanese lady whom I have forsaken almost fifty years ago and to whom I'm dying to extend my belated apologies and explanation before I expire, if I could by any remotest chance. Unlike you, I've usually been an unrealistic and impractical person except as to this lady, which became my lifelong regret and shame. I don't know if there is a similar saying in Japan as in Korea: "Make sure you build a Great Wall with a lady even if you sleep with her only for one night." In 1970, I visited Japan for the first time to attend a business conference in Tokyo. Capitalizing on my off-duty free time for a couple of days, I went to Kyoto and Nara for sightseeing after visiting the Osaka Expo. Upon arriving at the Kyoto train station, I approached a young lady in the plaza and, making use of my poor Japanese, I asked her for some directions. As it turned out, she was at the train station to meet her sister, and, saying goodbye to her sister, to my infinite surprise, she offered to be my guide for the day. How could I resist this undreamed of "romantic tour" with such an attractive lady? As if in a sweet dream, the whole day passed by in a blink of an eye. Even more surprising was her kind invitation for dinner at her home. After dinner with her and her friends, she accompanied me to the station. She even came down onto the platform to see me off after buying me some cookies and candies from the gift shop. I was taking the night train for Tokyo to fly back to Seoul the next morning. During the short flight, I was in agony, not knowing what to do. It may have been just a friendly goodwill kindness on her part, nothing more and nothing less. But as far as I was concerned, this was a case of "all or nothing" and "now or never." I did not let her know that I was a married man with two children. Since she didn't ask me, I felt it'd be presumptuous and rude of me to tell her I was not available. More likely, rather, unconsciously or subconsciously, how I wished I was a "free man!" After much struggle between my head and my heart, just moments before disembarking from the plane, I tore up and threw away the note she handed me with her name and address written on it. I justified and rationalized my action by telling myself: "It's all for her. I don't want to give her any 'false hope.' The sooner she forgets about me, the better off she will be to find a suitable, unattached bachelor." *Burning that bridge to her once and for all had to be the best decision that I could make for her, even though it was the worst for me,* I thought.

Tragi-comically enough, soon after my return home, my wife and I got divorced due to our irreconcilable differences. Our marriage was an accident in the first place. We had sex under the influence of alcohol one night without having had a date. In those days, "one-night-stand" was unheard of. I felt responsible and we married. As soon as we got divorced, we learned that she was pregnant with our third child. So we remarried for the sake of the children. After trying harder for eighteen more years, we got divorced again for the second time, twenty years after our first wedding.

In my earliest days, I started devouring great people's biographies and reciting their sayings. Thus, brainwashed and hypnotized, I convinced myself that I was a big fire, not a small one easily extinguished even by a breeze, like an eternal star that starts to shine as soon as the sky is dark enough, or like a kite that rises highest against the wind, not with it.

I forced myself to live by "sollen" ("ought to be" in German). However, I've come to realize, only after so many trials and errors, that one cannot go against the nature of things that is "sein" (just "to be" in German). What will happen, will; what will not, won't, no matter what. I've come to the conclusion that for anything to happen anytime anywhere, the whole Cosmos has to conspire.

If I had failed to build the Great Wall of our blink-brief romance half a century ago, I pray, with your assistance, I might be able to rebuild the bridge between us, at long last—even if it may be between our tombstones with a copy of the Japanese edition of my last book, Cosmian Rhapsody, laid at hers for a bouquet, my 26th and the very first in Japanese, if you are so kindly inclined to translate this book in English to be out in 2020.

Gratefully,
Lee Tae-Sang

9. Cosmian Is the Personification of Childlike Divinity

Asked in a recent interview with The Entertainment/Sports of The Korea Times, December 13, 2018, "If there is a tao running through your life as an artist, what would that be?" Korean singer-songwriter Lee Sang Eun a.k.a. Lee-Tzsche answered: "Not to lose the childlike innocence. The moment I lose it, I lose everything, all my perceptions, means of empathy." Wow, what a convincing, ever-lasting and universal testimony! Shouldn't this be the tao for every human being? That is to say, like the child in Hans Christian Andersen's "The Emperor's New Clothes" and Antoine de Saint Exupéry's fairy tale for grownups "The Little Prince/(Princess)."

"Do Children Need Religion?" by Martha Fay was published in 1994. The author, an ex-Catholic, of this book with its quizzical title, doesn't give clear-cut answers. She tells how she responds to the questions of her young (then only ten-year-old) daughter, Anna, about a She or a He God, a black or a white God, death, Heaven, the meaning of right and wrong, and the like.

Ever since my youngest days, I was disgusted by all the self-righteous dogmatism full of hypocrisy constantly exhibited by grownups. I kept telling myself that I would never grow up to be like that. When I became a father, I named my three daughters Hae-a (Child of the Sea), Su-a (Child of the Sky) and Song-a (Child of the Star) with the common letter "아" in Korean and "兒" in Chinese character, meaning "child," praying that they would never lose their childlike curiosity, enthusiasm, innocence, and sense of wonder. I, for one, believe that the child in us is the most divine "god-ling." Didn't Jesus say we couldn't enter heaven unless we were childlike? To a child, nothing is true or false, good or bad, beautiful or ugly, right or wrong, high or low, male or female; you and I are not separate, not separate from animals, plants or rocks. For, literally, all things in Nature are one and the same.

If the God of the sky is up there and the God of the earth is down here in the ground, children are those very Gods that descended down and ascended up. If anywhere children are, there is the very Heaven, if so, what Heaven up there in the sky or what Hell down in the underground could there be? If children are founders of religions, how could then anyone dare to preach to the godlings!

If God is oneness, so are the children as Little Cosmians.

10. Now I Must Become Myself

In order to extend my deeply felt thanks and best wishes to you all for the New Year, I am writing this short note.

Firstly, I'd like to share with you a couple of quotes below.

In an opinion page column article entitled "December Face" (Korea Daily/Joongang Ilbo, December 15, 2018) Ms. Ko Sun-hee, Broadcast Screenwriter/Scripter/Scenarist & Seoul Institute of the Arts Professor, quotes a phrase from "Now I Become Myself" by American poet May Sarton (1912-1995, the pen name of Eleanore Marie Sarton), after saying that the pure Korean word "얼굴(face)," a combination of two words "얼(soul)" and "굴(cave)," meaning, therein lies one's soul, the root of one's mind:
Now I Become Myself

Now I become myself, it's taken
Time, many years and places;
I have been dissolved and shaken,
Worn other people's faces,

There's a popular phrase in English, "Mind over Body," which I interpret as follows:

Your mind affects not only the health of your body, but it also affects the peace of your mind. In Buddhism, don't they put it this way, "Everything depends on the mind?" And Buddha was quoted as saying: "With our thoughts, we make the world."

"Eyes are windows of your mind and face is the map as well as the mirror of your life journey...by your facial expression alone, you tell how you've been leading your own life... You can get rid of all the wrinkles by cosmetic/plastic surgery, but you can never blind the windows of your soul."

This is a quote from "Father Wants to Leave Home Every Day," a nonfiction book by Kim Hee-gon published in Korea in 2010.

Since my early childhood, I was always amazed by how grownups, especially aged grandmas and grandpas, could judge a person's character by taking a quick glance at the person. As I have come to age, I too have come to recite the old adage "by looking at a bit (sample) of the behavior of a person, you can tell all about that person."

As you may all know, The Secret, a best-selling 2006 self-help book by Rhonda Byrne that has sold 30 million copies worldwide and has been translated into 50 languages is based on the belief of the law of attraction.

If I were to summarize the message of this book in a phrase, it could be "Like Attracts Like." Your positive attitude will bring about a positive outcome. Didn't Pablo Picasso say, "Everything you can imagine is real?"

Something I want to get across to you, based on my own life experience of living and observing people around me for 82 years, is that sometimes things that you have never even dreamed of and that you could never have even imagined can happen, indeed, like miracles, or rather, more than miracles, beyond all belief. One example is the birth of Cosmian News. Ha—Ha—Really.

All of us are briefly sojourning on this global village of planet earth, mind you, each and every one. "Now I (Must) Become Myself," just like the title of May Sarton's poem quoted above. This very "Myself" is none other than "Cosmian," I pray.

December 16, 2018
Lee Tae-Sang

11. Nostalgia for Analog

Vitamin water® is offering $100,000 if you can stay off smartphones for a year.

To enter the contest, you need to submit a post on Twitter or Instagram (so, yes, perhaps using a smartphone), including the hashtags #nophoneforayear and #contest, and outlining what you'd do if you couldn't swipe or scroll for a year. The deadline to enter is January 8, 2019.

The company will select a contestant around January 22, according to the contest rules, and give them a 1996-era cell phone. For the next year, if you get chosen, you can't use any smartphones or tablets at all, even those belonging to other people, but you can use laptops and desktop computers. Devices like Google Home and Amazon Echo are OK too.

If you can go a full year carrying around something like what Cher used in the iconic teen comedy "Clueless," you'll win $100,000. If you last six months, you get $10,000.

Oh, and Vitaminwater® will be verifying your honesty. Before receiving the money, the contestant will need to submit to a lie-detector test.

Vitaminwater® likes challenging monotony, Natalia Suarez, the company's associate brand manager, tells CNBC Make It. "We don't think there's anything more boring than mindlessly scrolling through your phone, and this is an opportunity to take that stance against routine and give someone $100,000 to do something uniquely awesome with their time," she says.

Reading this news as reported on December 13, 2018, by Megan Leonhardt @Megan_Leonhardt CNBC.com, I was overcome with acute nostalgia for my analog days in my youth.

What I read in my teens in an article has been incubating in my mind, or in my heart, ever since.

The writer of the article posited that silent, black and white movies are better than those of technicolor with soundtracks; novels are better than films; poems are better than novels, for each of the viewers or readers can exercise freely one's infinite imagination about the colors, figures, voices of all the characters, and sights and sounds of all the scenes.

This argument seems to be in the same vein as claims that clothed women are much more attractive, mysteriously more beautiful than naked ones; the unspoken words left unsaid are more convincing and lasting than those spelled out; hand-written correspondence is more touching than a telephone conversation.

American essayist/philosopher Ralph Waldo Emerson (1803-1882) must have meant the same when he said:

"Use what language you will, you can never say anything but what you are."

Then, perchance, the old-fashioned arranged marriages and romancing by long, long love-letters are much more intimate and enduring than the current lightning quick "speed dating" scene.

Soundless music, wordless communion, and unseen vision, and the like may overcome all our senses, time and space, even life and death, to boot, perhaps.

Who's to say the ideal is not meant to be realized?

12. *Bohemian Rhapsody Is Cosmian Cantata*

"Bohemian Rhapsody" is a musical film about the British rock band Queen and its lead singer Freddie Mercury. It is a worldwide hit, watched by more than six million people in South Korea alone, it was recently reported.

Freddie is described as having "defied stereotypes and shattered convention to become one of the most beloved entertainers on the planet."

Let's think about the conventional wisdom of following the crowd, called a convention, custom, and tradition, mindlessly just "going with the flow," so to speak.

It is usually said that tradition is something long-established; convention is a traditional method or style of behaving that is considered to be correct or polite by most people in a society, and custom is a traditional and widely accepted way of behaving or doing something that is specific to a particular society, place, or time.

Bohemian derives from Bohemia, the westernmost and largest historical region of the Czech lands in the present-day Czech Republic and denotes the lifestyle or the people of living an artistic, open-minded, unconventional and unencumbered life.

Throughout human history all over the world, most people have been bound by all kinds of boundaries, such as class, nationality, race, sex, imposed by ideology, politics, and religion. They have been misled and influenced by mob psychology.

To cite a few examples, they are the "original sin," the "chosen people," black and white mindset/white supremacy, sex discrimination, sexual orientation, witch hunt, chastity belt, female genital mutilation, feet binding, honor killing, ethnic cleansing/genocide, etc., such as colonialism and slavery.

All these most horrendous, inhuman and unnatural barbarities have been in practice due to our failure to realize that we are born boundless as Cosmians.

So, let's sing along our Cosmian Cantata altogether, now and forever.

13. "Toxic" Human
Vs "Cosmic" Cosmian

"Toxic" was chosen by Oxford Dictionaries as the international word of 2018, apparently reflecting the current toxic human—economic, environmental, political, sexual and societal—climate of the world, taking notice of the #MeToo movement triggered by "toxic masculinity" in particular. This English word "toxic," I'm told, comes from the Greek "toxikon pharmakon," meaning "poison for arrows." (The part of the phrase meaning arrows, rather than poison, is said to have become the basis for the word, though.) Initially, for its first few centuries, it literally meant poisonous plants but gradually its meaning expanded metaphorically to indicate anything harmful and deadly.

As there are toxic or nourishing food and drinks, it's the same with people, isn't it? Therefore, one should keep the toxic away and stick to what's good for one's body and soul.

Also, as there are two different courses of treatment in medical terminology, namely, "symptomatic therapy" that only affects its symptoms, not its cause, i.e., its etiology and "radical therapy" that intends to cure, not palliate. They say that eastern medicine treats the roots while western medicine treats the outgrowth, believe it or not. If so, likewise, the best treatment for all our ailments, problems, troubles and whatnot, must be to open up our innate cosmic vision for our expanded and extended self-realization as Cosmians, being "cosmic," way above and beyond being chaotic and toxic, no more. Hence, the #MeToo movement must be advanced to the #UsAll Cosmian movement so that our current chaotic world will turn into the most beautiful and wonderful Cosmos as it was meant to be and, let's pray, "Cosmian" will be chosen as the most becoming word of 2019 or '2020.'

14. HQ or Rather CQ
to Be Enhanced

People say that a high IQ will help you to go to college or to get the job you want. But how successful you will be is going to be decided by your EQ. This word EQ is said to have been first coined by Harvard psychologist Daniel Goleman (b. 1946) in his 1955 book "Emotional Intelligence," which became The New York Times bestseller. It was recently reported that by nationality, Korea ranked 1st in the world with its average IQ of 106, according to "Race Differences in Intelligence" authored by British psychologist Richard Lynn (b. 1930), based on his almost 50-year-research studies. Korea was followed by Japan with 105, Taiwan with 104, Germany with 102, China with 100, the U.S.A. with 98 and Israel with 94. IQ was first used, we are told, by German psychologist William Stern, born Ludwig Wilhelm Stern (1871-1938) in German, which was adopted into English. And the word "Intelligence" is said to derive from an Indo-European word meaning "gather, collect," to which "inter" that indicates "between, middle" was added as a prefix. Besides IQ and EQ, SQ (Spiritual Quotient) has been in general use in some quarters in recent years. Be that as it may, in order to live a happy life as a human being, regardless of nationality, race, sex or social class, one has to enhance, above all, one's HQ (Humanity Quotient) and furthermore NQ (Nature Quotient), that is, our common cosmic vision CQ (Cosmic/Cosmian Quotient), encompassing us all as Cosmians born Arainbow of Love.

15. An Open Letter to Ms. Liane Moriarty

The best-selling author of Big Lies.

Dear Ms. Liane Moriarty,

Reading your interview article with Ms. Belinda Luscombe of TIME Nov. 26/Dec. 3, 2018, I'm prompted to take the liberty of writing this unsolicited open letter to you. Please kindly understand my sincere intent to commiserate with all the poor souls including myself (early in my life), still imprisoned in the arbitrary dungeon of the Dark Age of the most inhuman and unnatural self-righteous religious dogma, full of falsehood and hypocrisy.

Asked In 10 Questions: The main character in your new novel, *Nine Perfect Strangers,* is a genre fiction writer who gets little respect. Is she a mouthpiece for you? You answered: A little bit. But I didn't want the book becoming a soapbox or preachy. But of course, because this character was close to my heart, she has feelings that would be similar to mine. Further asked: In some ways, *Nine Perfect Strangers* reminded me of the Stanford Prison Experiment, where "inmates" did what they were told even when it seemed inhuman. Why do we do what we're told? You answered: For this book, I read about Jonestown, so I did want to give that feeling of being in a cult. We're all basically obedient. I think that the desire to be someone new is so strong that it's easy to believe the most ridiculous things. Asked again: This novel explores what people think about when they're facing death. Do you think that reflects your Catholic [uncatholic] school education? You answered: I don't like to analyze how much of myself goes into my books. The fact that little parts of myself might find their way into these stories—it's mortifying, to be honest. But I definitely have that Catholic feeling of guilt; I feel guilty about my success. In the early days, I used to think, *You're going to pay for this; something terrible will happen next.* Nothing has yet. But if it does, I'll think, *Well, there you go; you deserve it.*

Unlike, or rather in stark contrast to, the *Nine Perfect Strangers*, the Nine Ladies of my book published in 2019, *Cosmian*, I trust, will enlighten, inspire and uplift us all, originally blessed cosmically as "Cosmians Arainbow."

Sincerely,
Lee Tae-Sang

16. How to Be Cosmian

Leftist or rightist, liberal or conservative, progressive or reactionary ideology; black or white racism; right or wrong, good or bad judgment; male and female, the chosen or heathen, upper or lower class, us or them mentality and mindset, etc.; all these divisive discriminations imprison us all earthlings, bound for self-destruction, forsaking win-win solution, causing the current climate change and all sorts of other human-made calamities and catastrophes, conflicts and disasters, wars and what not.

If so, what would be more imperative and urgent than to be awakened to appreciate the experience being born arainbow of love through the union of our parents on this most beautiful and wonderful planet earth as brief sojourners to return to the Cosmos, to be aware of our true identity as Cosmians to share our common cosmic vision in living and loving during our short stay here on earth? In order to come to this realization, every one of us has to be enlightened and inspired to learn that one is not separate from each other, being a microcosmos reflecting the whole of the macrocosmos, all that existed in the past, all that exists at present and all that will exist in the future. Thus, we're all in it together, all on our separate, uplifting journeys to realize that loving someone or something is loving oneself and the whole of the Cosmos itself.

May each one of us be the Sea of Cosmos!

17. How to Become an Optimist

Nietzsche urges us to be wanderers, "Though not as a traveler to a final destination: for, this destination does not exist."

Nevertheless, young Nietzsche instructs:

"Set for yourself goals, high and noble goals, and perish in pursuit of them."

This means that what can be achieved cannot be your ideal. Doesn't it?

If Nietzsche is an idealist, Epictetus may be called a realist. A version of the story by the Ancient Greek Stoic philosopher, who was born a slave, goes:

"I have to die. If it is now, well, then, I die now; if later, then now I will take my lunch, since the hour for lunch has arrived—and dying I will tend to later."

I recall what Nora says in "From Prada to Nada," a 2011 US romantic comedy film based on Jane Austin's 1811 novel "Sense and Sensibility"—when the spoiled sisters Nora and Mary have to move in with their Aunt Aurelia in East L.A.'s Boyle Heights after their world of wealth and privilege in Beverly Hills crashes, following their father's sudden death.

When asked how she is doing, Nora replies:

"Well, you know, like a cockroach, I can accommodate anything and thrive anywhere."

So, perhaps, one can say that when looked at from the big picture, everything is trivial, has two sides, and is just beautiful and wonderful.

Although to be an idealist or a realist is one's choice, at the same time, by combining the two, one can become an optimist.

18. To the Successful by the Virtue of Competence and Endeavor

(Originally published in *The Cosmian News*, both in English and in Korean on August 21, 2018.)

"Success and Luck: Good Fortune and The Myth of Meritocracy" by Robert H. Frank that came out in 2017 was recently translated and published in Korean, entitled "To the Successful by the Virtue of Competence and Endeavor." In this book, the author, a professor of economics at Cornell University, argues that the successful tend to underestimate the role that chance plays. The issue is whether it's hard work or luck that decides the outcome. This may sound like there's no other option, but I'd like to present the third option one can take. Whatever and how many options there are, what you decide to take is up to your choice. Isn't it?

All the while living my life for eighty-odd years, I've never even dreamed that there would be a day like today, one day. Looking back, had I not lost my first love almost sixty years ago, I could not have come to realize that I, and all others, all beings are "cosmians" born "arainbow" from the Cosmos. A young boy who happened to fall in love with the microcosmos of a flower ended up embracing the whole macrocosmos.

Although everyone encounters from time to time both blessings and curses in disguise, doesn't it make all the difference depending, no matter whether it's a "fortune" or a "misfortune," on what one makes it to be, after all. We see all the time the fall of the most powerful and successful from the pinnacle of power and success, while some "hopeless" and "helpless" losers rise from the ashes of despair and failures, like a phoenix.

I'd like to share a bit of my most recent experience. Following the publication of two books in September 2017, "39 Project" and "Tae-Mi Sa-Byun (Dialectic Dialogue— Thought Romance Between An 80-Year-Old Man and A 24-Year-Old Girl)," I commissioned this very promising young entrepreneur who had pulled off these two great surprise feats of publishing success to launch a new quarterly "Cosmian" in the same spirit and vein of the now-defunct very popular intellectual monthly magazine "Ssassanggye" (The World of Thoughts) in March 2018. Although this project was aborted, it was replaced by another much more meaningful and visionary global online daily newspaper, The Cosmian News *http://www.cosmiannews.com*, which was launched on July 10, 2018. In 2018, my Korean publisher, Ms. Jeon Seungseon, Poet, Novelist, and Playwright, started writing a nonfiction narrative of my life, "Cosmian" (in Korean), and it was published on June 1, 2018. So I contacted Ms. Deborah Smith, the English translator of Korean novelist Han Kang's novel "The Vegetarian," which won The Man

Booker International Prize in 2016. Since my approach was unsuccessful, I decided to translate it into English myself, revising and rewriting it in my own words.

Furthermore, a Cosmian Festival in celebration of the inauguration of The Cosmian News was held in Seoul, Korea, on October 27, 2018. On October 19, 2019, the First Annual Cosmian Prize was awarded to the top two non-fiction narrative essay contest winners with 7 million won (Korean currency, equivalent to about US $7,000) for the grand prize and 3 million won for the gold prize. The Second Annual Cosmian Prize will be awarded in October 2020. And the Second Cosmian Festival will take place in Pyongchang , Korea, in the fall of 2020, on the campus of Cosmian University at its inauguration, Cosmos willing. Cosmian University may include Cosmian School of Music and Cosmian Orchestra, again Cosmos willing. I do agree with Buddha:

"With our thoughts, we make the world."

A new album, Cosmian Song: As Heart Beats by Korean singer-songwriter, Navid, popular in China, Japan, and Korea, was issued on June 30, 2019. The lyrics of the title song of the album was written by Ms. Jeon Seungseon.

Therefore, as the saying goes, if not this, someone or something far better will turn up, sooner or later, if one never ceases to look for what one wants. I'm reminded of a comment confided by the late V. S. Naipaul (1932-2018), winner of the 2001 Nobel Prize for Literature, who was born in Trinidad in a family with Indian roots and just passed away.

"I knew the door I wanted, I knocked." He must have meant to say that there are so many doors. If one door

doesn't open, I'll knock another. If another door still doesn't, I'll knock yet another until one opens. At the same time, we'd better recall Steve Jobs' motto:

"The journey (itself) is the reward." It is tough to accept the hard truths of life but we all have to accept them anyway. One is that for anything to happen anytime anywhere, the whole Cosmos has to conspire. Won't it be? Anyway, I concur with Tony Morrison:

"At some point in life world's beauty becomes enough."

19. *Art or Life*

On October 25, 2018, the portrait of Edmond Belamy, the first piece of AI-generated art to come to auction at Christie's, was sold for $432,500, signaling the arrival of AI art on the world auction stage. This is no news in the light of the fact that novels are already being written and musical instruments are being played by AI. Furthermore, professional jobs performed by highly paid-physicians, lawyers, stockbrokers, etc., are gradually going to be replaced by much more accurate, efficient and cheaper services rendered by AI. As Irish Nobel Prize-winning writer George Bernard Shaw (1856-1950) remarked, "All professions are conspiracies against the laity," this trend may be direly deplored by all the heretofore culturally and socially privileged aristocrats. But this should be greeted gleefully by grassroots! Edifices like Egyptian Pyramids, Greek and Roman Pantheons and Colosseums, European Cathedrals, Chinese Great Wall, Indian and other Asian Hindu/Buddhist temples, etc., have been treasured as great assets of cultural heritage. Nevertheless, alas, one cannot forget the hard facts that so many slaves and laborers were sacrificed for them, with the connivance of high priests and monks.

Come to think of it all, there are no more miraculously wonderful "nature facts" than nature as it is, and no greater "artifacts" than life as lived in earnest, breath by breath. If so, how then could one worship the imitated images of nature and life, pursuing the shadows instead of here-and-now entities? I'm not sure where and when I noticed this sentence: "Art is what makes life more interesting than the art itself." I'd interpret this as to mean that there is no other artist than "the artist of life itself."

A few years ago, the daughter of a colleague of mine, an Arabic court interpreter, lost her newlywed husband on their honeymoon, while taking a photograph of him standing on a rock against the roaring sea. Therefore, perhaps, one has to say that reality is so much stranger than virtual reality and that Nature is infinitely greater than any human achievements.

These two quotes offer contrasting perspectives for us to puzzle over:

"There is nothing greater than the joy of composing something oneself and then listening to it.

My imagination can picture no fairer happiness than to continue living for art."

– Clara Schumann

"If I had written the greatest book, composed the greatest symphony, painted the most beautiful painting or carved the most exquisite figure, I could not have felt the more exalted creator than I did when they placed my child in my arms.

No human creature could receive or contain so vast a flood of love and joy as I often felt after the birth of my child. With this came the need to worship, to adore."

– Dorothy Day

20. Intoxication and Detoxicant

As another year is coming to a close, people tend to have more occasions to drink in gatherings of scattered family members, alumni, and friends.

Roman historian Tacitus (Pablius Cornelius Tacitus, C. 55-A.D. 117) recorded:

Ancient Germanic tribes would hold wartime negotiations drunk, reasoning that it made all parties incapable of hiding anything.

When drunk, one often becomes "not oneself, not like her/him," under the influence of alcohol, sometimes causing extraordinary accidents. This may be due to the disarmament of the drunkard to expose her/his so far concealed true color and nature to the world.

One can be intoxicated, not only with alcohol, nicotine or drug but more prevalently and predominantly with political, religious and social ideologies. Lo and behold, as long as humanity is gripped by this "black and white" false dichotomy, the world cannot help being a "living hell" for so many underprivileged people.

The only panacea detoxicant for this deadly intoxication is none other than "love." Won't it be? What then is this "love?"

Let's reflect upon what Toni Morrison (1931-2019), the American writer who was awarded the Nobel Prize in Literature in 1993, says:

"Everybody remembers the first time they were taught that part of the human race was Other… It's as though I told you that your left hand is not part of your body."

The above-quoted two sentences, at first, sound like they are contradicting each other. However, on second thought, it is easily understood that the first statement goes without saying, needless to say.

So, if one truly loves oneself and one's whole body, one has to love and respect every part of it, each cell of the part, head to toe, she must have made this eternal self-help home truth abundantly clear.

21. "Übermensch" Is "Cosmian"

Edward Gorey (1925-2000), the American writer and artist noted for his illustrated books was quoted as saying:

"Explaining something makes it go away."

I'd interpret this as to mean that just the words alone without action are in vain.

If those who draw in letters are writers, those who write in drawings are artists, those who paint in sound are musicians, what should we call those who draw, paint, and write in living, especially those who live in loving?

Nietzsche challenges us "to become who you are." He must be urging us to be "Übermensch."

Man, "인간" in Korean and "人間" in Chinese characters, is the abbreviation for "인생세간" in Korean and "人生世間" in Chinese characters, the world where s/he lives between "천계" in Korean and "天界" in Chinese meaning "the heavenly world" and "하계" in Korean and "下界" in Chinese meaning "the nether world."

If so, then there must be a clear message in Nietzsche's Übermensch that one has to soar into the Sky/Sea of Cosmos, after a short stay on earth, leaving one's shell of the body behind in dust or ashes.

That's the way to become what we are, Cosmians!

22. *Cyborg Is Cosmian*

"Cyborg" is an abbreviation for "cybernetic organism," meaning the combination of an organism and inorganic/inanimate matter like machines.

As Tesla CEO Elon Musk (b. 1971) declared on June 2, 2016, we're all "already cyborgs," nowadays, we're living in the so-called "Hyper-Connected" society through the internet network. Aren't we?

From time immemorial, our ancestors (in the East) practiced "축지법(chukjipob)" in Korean alphabet and "縮地法" in Chinese characters: "a method of making a long distance close in by the magic of contracting space."

Since machines like bicycles, automobiles, and airplanes were invented, not only the distance over the land but also over the water of rivers and oceans were contracted by ships and balloons. These days, even the space of the universe/multiverse is being abridged. Isn't it?

I can't help recalling an episode in my youth. In 1959 when I graduated from college, I met my first love, whom I started calling my Cosmos, a symbol of my favorite flower cosmos representing the whole Cosmos.

One day, we went to see a film, The Brothers Karamazov. Waiting in the second-floor lobby for the next showing, she asked me if I wanted to go to the bathroom. I didn't feel like going, but I went anyway. The entrances to the men's and women's bathrooms were side by side. I stood for a moment in front of the urinal and a thought crossed my mind that I and my Cosmos were not far apart with only a wall between us. I realized if the distance was shortened by just a few feet, I could be in her. At the very moment, I experienced the contraction of the space. Thereafter, I never felt lonesome again. Anytime, anywhere, I could feel close to anybody. If the whole universe were compressed into a single dot, one could be united with all. No doubt, this must have been a foresight of what's to come.

Come to think of it further, would "organism" be really so different from inorganic/inanimate matter?

In most recent years, organ transplants became no more unusual, and medical surgeries, housekeeping chores, etc., are being done more efficiently by robots. Even sex partners are being replaced by robots, believe it or not. A few days ago, it was reported that DNA-edited twins were born in China.

Besides, we are familiar with the phenomena, such as ESP (extra sensory perception) telepathy, precognition/foresight dream, NDE (near-death experience) and the like, which cannot be explained by science.

That's why, I gather, Sir Isaac Newton (1643-1767) sighed:

"I do not know what I may appear to the world; but to myself, I seem to have been only like a boy playing on the seashore, and diverting myself in now and then finding a

smoother pebble or a prettier shell than ordinary, whilst the great ocean of truth lay all undiscovered before me."

Likewise, perhaps, one can have no choice but to soliloquize:

All things in the Cosmos, no matter whether they appear to be breathing organisms or inorganic/inanimate matter that seems to have stopped breathing, are none other than "I" myself, the microcosm of the Cosmos, namely, Cosmian.

23. Meeting Devoid of Attraction Is No Meeting At All

It's called "chemistry" in English, which may be translated into Korean as "궁합," meaning astrological, carnal and personality compatibility. This is to say that there has to be an attraction between you and whom you meet and what you do. Otherwise, there cannot be real love and passion to speak of.

It is a new trend in the United States of America these days that airlines, restaurants and other businesses are suffering from "no-shows" and "ghosting"—such as failing to come to an interview, to report to work or quitting the job without giving notice.

Under the headline "Workers are ghosting their employers like bad dates," Danielle Paquette of The Washington Post, December 12, 2018, reported that workers are ditching jobs with nary a text.

How come this is happening?

The answer could be given in a word: loss of humanity for lack of a better word. In our modern capitalistic and technological society run by all-business-logic, no room is left for human relationships and touch that can be nurtured by companionship, friendship, esprit de corps, etc.

When you feel you are just being exploited by the system, how can you develop love and passion for anybody or anything? One can be immersed in romance or one's work only when you are totally attracted to someone or something. Then, only then, you can give it all, your life and whatnot.

Only then, one can recite a poem by William Blake (1757-1827) as one's own:

To see a World in a Grain of Sand
And a Heaven in a Wild Flower.
Hold Infinity in the palm of your hand
And Eternity in an hour.

24. Meteor Is Starshit

In Korean, a meteor is literally called "starshit," though it is called a falling or shooting star in English.

In Korean, the jobless are called "백(white)수(hands)," meaning clean, unsoiled and empty-handed. Nowadays, it's a worldwide phenomenon that young people, the ivory-towered college-educated in particular, cannot find jobs because they avoid 3D—dangerous, difficult and dirty—ones, while small businesses cannot fill the void.

In my childhood, when I came home from school, I was busy tending the vegetable garden, fetching shit as fertilizer from our shitshack. In the 1940s, the modern-day flush toilet was unheard of. One day, I fell into a shitpond in the field, chasing after dragonflies for summer vacation homework, and dog-swam out of it. This remains the sweetest memory I cherish all my life.

Let's ponder over the natural phenomenon that when snow and ice melt, they become dewdrops and raindrops; when water evaporates, it becomes clouds and mist. Likewise, truth to be told, what we eat turns into shit. Otherwise, we cannot live. Can we?

I'd like to share a fable from "THE FORERUNNER" (1920) by Kahlil Gibran (1883-1931)

"Said a Sheet of Snow-White Paper..."

Said a sheet of snow-white paper, "Pure was I created, and pure will I remain forever. I would rather be burnt and turn to white ashes than suffer darkness to touch me or the unclean to come near me."

The ink bottle heard what the paper was saying, and it laughed in its dark heart, but it never dared to approach her. And the multicolored pencils heard her also, and they too never came near her.

And the snow-white sheet of paper did remain pure and chaste for ever—pure and chaste—and empty.

After all, aren't we Cosmians nothing but stardust scattered by starshit?

25. We All Are Masked Singing Cosmians

American version of "THE MASKED SINGER," the new weekly singing competition show that will keep everyone guessing! "See who's behind the mask" premiered January 2, 2019, on FOX. This show is modeled after the original Korean one.

Come to think of it, we all are "masked singers." Aren't we? People put on all kinds of clothes, makeup and masks all the time, not only different nationalities, races, sexes, but also blinding ideologies, politics, religions, depriving us of our true humanity.

That's why Thomas Paine (1737-1809), (Spiritual) Founding Father of the United States, must have declared:

"My country is the world, and my religion is to do good."

No matter where one is born, where one is from, whether from the East, the West, the North or the South, it doesn't and shouldn't matter. If we look at things from the big picture, we all are "cosmians" born "arainbow" of love, on this tiny leaf-boat-like planet earth as fleeting sojourners for a picnic and then to sail on in the sea of cosmos. So we've got to sing our Cosmos Cantata all together.

May each one of us, be it a dewdrop or raindrop, be it a snowflake or a mist of cloud, trickle into the Sea of Cosmos, snuggling with our Eternal Mother!

26. I'm Incomplete, So I Like It

"Don't be ashamed to be a human being, be proud!
Inside you, one vault after another opens endlessly.
You'll never be complete, and that's as it should be."
– Swedish poet Tomas Transtromer (1931-2015)

This reminds me of a saying by the American philosopher William James (1842-1910):

"Most people live in a very restricted circle of their potential being. They make use of a very small portion of their possible consciousness, and of their soul's resources in general, much like a man who, out of his whole organism should get into a habit of using and moving only his little finger."

Where there are human shortcomings and weaknesses, there also are human touches and virtues, as though fish cannot live in too clean water. Some people say that Heaven will be too boring and that Hell will be all the more interesting.

When we are faced with adversities, we can exert our hidden and sometimes even superhuman power that we were not aware existed in us and turn them into blessings in disguise. Don't we?

Were we designed and programmed to be "perfect" like robots, what challenge, fun, joy, and thrill would we have? Would that life be worth living at all? Were we to know what would happen tomorrow or in the next (?) life, what an essential banality there would be to the life we live today?

How fortunate and lucky we are to be born half-divine and half-beastly, as a hybrid of god and animal, free to exercise an option to upgrade or downgrade ourselves!

There are two kinds of teachers in the world. Good teachers show good examples but greater lessons and warning signs are given by those who fail themselves. So, we should really feel more grateful to the latter for their sacrifices.

Thus looked at, all things seem to be O.K., don't they? So we are just fine as we are. Perchance, utopia is not meant to be reached here and now.

27. Self-Love/Respect Completes Oneself

"If your compassion does not include yourself, it is incomplete."

This quote from Jack Kornfield (b. 1945), American Buddhist Practitioner and one of the key teachers to introduce Buddhist mindfulness practice to the West recalls the age-old saying of "charity begins at home." This saying derives from a sentence in "Martin Chuzzlewit," one of works by English novelist Charles Dickens (1812-1870): "Charity begins at home and justice begins next door." This sentence may be understood to mean either that I do care only about my well-being and the laws and the like are none of my business, or that love begins at home and justice starts in society, paraphrasing a saying by English churchman Thomas Fuller (1608-1661): "Charity begins at home, but should not end there." We say in the East "수신제가 치국평천하" in Korean and "修身齊家治國平天下" in Chinese characters, meaning "Take care of your family first and then mind the business of the world later." However, it rings so true as American novelist James Baldwin (1924-1987) laments: "Incontestably, alas, most people are not, in action, worth very much; and yet, every human being is an unprecedented miracle. One tries to treat them as the miracles they are while trying to protect oneself against the disasters they've become." Isn't this the very message of the current worldwide #MeToo Movement?

This message is summed up succinctly in two short sentences, or rather two words: "Empathy is the antidote to shame… The most powerful words when we're in struggle: me too."—by Dr. Brene Brown (b. 1965), who is a research professor at the University of Houston where she holds the Huffington-Brene Brown Endowed Chair at The Graduate College of Social Work. Be that as it may, meanwhile, we can be comforted and even exhilarated by what the English comedian Stephen Fry (b. 1957) says: "Heightened self-consciousness, apartness, an inability to join in, physical shame, self-loathing—they are not all bad. Those devils have also been my angels. Without them, I would never have disappeared into language, literature, the mind, laughter, and all the mad intensities that made and unmade me."

So, perhaps, there is nothing to be discarded, after all as long as one cares to love and respect oneself and all others as other-selves of oneself.

28. Pro-Human Is
Pro-Heaven and Earth

Snowflakes can be deceiving. Banksy transformed them from a marker of winter festivities into a symbol of the plague of air pollution in his mural Seasons greetings in Port Talbot, Wales, thus reported. (https://www.lifegate.com)

The phrase "pros and cons" is an abbreviation of the Latin phrase "pro et contra," "for and against," and has been in use in the abbreviated form since the 16th century, according to the Oxford English Dictionary.

Another commonly used phrase "philes and phobias" is a love-hate thing. The two suffixes -phile and -phobia are very nearly opposite in meaning. The suffix -phile is from the Greek word philia, meaning friendship. A word ending in -phile indicates someone having great fondness or preference for something. In contrast to -phile, -phobia indicates a strong, unreasonable, or abnormal fear or dislike of something, according to Saddlespace.org.

According to Urban Dictionary, weirdly enough, anthrophilia means sexual attraction to non-human but humanoid creatures. Extreme case of anthrophilia causes the impure to disregard gender when it comes to their sexual preference and may cause them to find human men/women boring in comparison, thereby removing sexuality from a human. And anthrophobia means fear of mankind or other people.

Anyway, no doubt, someone like the anonymous England-based street artist, vandal, political activist, and film director known as Banksy is a pro-human, pro-earth and pro-heaven, namely Cosmosphile and Chaosphobiac. What's so great, courageous and admirable of him is he is acting upon his conviction as the conscience of humanity.

29. To See a Flicker of Eternity in Moments

"In losing my future, the mundane began to sparkle."

This is what Kate Bowler says, an associate professor at Duke Divinity School, the author of Everything Happens for a Reason: And Other Lies I've Loved. She found out at age 35 that she had stage IV cancer, having had finally had a baby son with her childhood sweetheart.

"Christian theology has rich categories for the future," she writes, "about the kingdom of God... But the sicker I became, the more "hope" was a word that pointed to the unbearable: a husband and a baby left behind, an end without an ending... As far as I was concerned, it poisoned the sacred work of living in the present."

Would this be the story of Kate alone? When we think about it, aren't we all, each and every one of us, terminal, born to die, sooner or later?

And yet, for tens of centuries, people have been brainwashed and indoctrinated that no matter what you do against humanity in this life, you can be redeemed only by the blood of somebody and enter the kingdom of God. It goes without saying that the "indulgences" and the "admission tickets" to Heaven are still being sold all over the world in all its various guises.

How and why people fail to get enlightened and realize that there is neither the past nor the future but the present; that how you live in the moment at present determines the past and the future; that when you like and love someone or something, you make the heaven on earth, whereas you bring about the hell on earth when you dislike and hate somebody or something; and that whether it's a person's look, landscape, seascape or skyscape, it changes constantly from moment to moment, one look or view only at a time, once for all, never to be repeated.

To borrow a sentence from Prof. Bowler's Opinion column article "Hope Isn't Only About the Future," published in The New York Times Sunday Review, December 30, 2018:

"This is transcendence, the past and the future experienced together in moments where I can see a flicker of eternity."

So it's perforce just "to see a flicker of eternity in moments."

30. What Do the Missing Vowels Mean?

There is a fashion in American language culture these days to be playful like children, leaving out the vowels in names, sentences, and words.

For example, the rock band that was originally named "The Management" is now simply called MGMT and tech companies like Tumblr and Flickr, are dropping e's. People are signing their (ever-briefer) correspondence "Yrs." They say that the first step in the stage of language's evolution, or rather devolution, has already happened.

How come? This may be reflecting the reality that nowadays, young people are avoiding marriage and having children.

From this trend, we can infer that missing vowels will be followed by missing consonants, and it will eventually lead to dispensing with language altogether.

Furthermore, if missing vowels mean missing Mother Nature, it will be followed by missing childhood, and consequently, the heaven on earth of childhood will disappear, while only living hell of adults will remain.

Not to be so pessimistic, I pray, good riddance to all the talk of love, equality, freedom, human rights and peace without walking the walk. This must be the divine revelation, that we should start living these ideals instead of just talking the talk in lip service.

In his sonnet "Vowels," the French poet Jean Nicolas Arthur Rimbaud (1854-1891) names the five vowels, linking each to a color: "A black, E white, I red, U green, O blue: Vowels." Although he continues in the second line of the poem, "I will someday tell of your latent birth," subsequently, in his work, Une Saison Enfer (A Season in Hell), he would write, "I invented the color of vowels! I withheld the translation of it."

Perhaps we can find the missing explanation in this short Rimbaud quote: "Genius is the recovery of childhood at will."

In retrospect, weren't we all born with the celestial divinity to enjoy our childhood before we learn to speak in any language?

31. The Phantom (?) of Art and Religion

In Korean, there is an expression mocking the self-chosen one as *"living on dewdrops and passing droppings of clouds."* Such a person believes that *"art is long and life is short"* or that *"religion is the only truth in life."*

There is a parable as a refreshing reminder for us all from The Forerunner by Kahlil Gibran (1883-1931): *Four poets were sitting around a bowl of punch that stood on a table. Said the first poet, "Methinks I see with my third eye the fragrance of this wine hovering in space like a cloud of birds in an enchanted forest." The second poet raised his head and said, "With my inner ear I can hear those mist-birds singing. And the melody holds my heart as the white rose imprisons the bee within her petals." The third poet closed his eyes and stretched his arm upwards, and said, "I touch them with my hand. I feel their wings, like the breath of a sleeping fairy, brushing against my fingers." Then the fourth poet rose and lifted up the bowl, and he said, "Alas, friends! I am too dull of sight and of hearing and of touch. I cannot see the fragrance of this wine, nor feel the beating of its wings. I perceive but the wine itself. Now, therefore, must I drink it, that it may sharpen my senses and raise me*

to your blissful heights." And putting the bowl to his lips,
he drank the punch to the last drop. The three poets, with
their mouths open, looked at him aghast, and there was a
thirsty yet unlyrical hatred in their eyes.

32. We All Are Mad People, If Not Clowns

American publishers are dealing with the #MeToo era by adding the increasingly widespread "morality clause" to their standard book contracts, and they can ask authors to return their advances.

In South Korea too, famous people from all walks of life, including the celebrated poet Ko Un, have been accused by the victims of their habitual sexual misconduct that have been connived at and tolerated by the general public as "open secrets" for far too long.

The worldwide scandal involving the clergy in recent years exposed those "holy" men of God as "wolves in lamb's clothing."

We'd better ruminate over what the Irish Nobel Prize-awarded playwright George Bernard Shaw (1856-1950) declared:

"All professions are conspiracies against the laity."

Besides, other socially looked-up people like physicians, especially those who treat the mentally ill, may enjoy this flippant remark:

"The neurotics build castles in the air, and the psychotics live in them, while the psychiatrists collect the rent."

Now let's hear what The Madman had to say in THE MADMAN, from "THE WANDERER: His Parables and Sayings" (1932) by Kahlil Gibran (1883-1931).

THE MADMAN

It was in the garden of a madhouse that I met a youth with a face pale and lovely and full of wonder.

And I sat beside him upon the bench, and I said, "Why are you here?"

And he looked at me in astonishment, and he said, "It is an unseemly question, yet I will answer. My father would make of me a reproduction of himself; so also would my uncle. My mother would have me the image of her illustrious father. My sister would hold up her seafaring husband as the perfect example for me to follow. My brother thinks I should be like him, a fine athlete.

"And my teachers also, the doctor of philosophy, and the music-master, and the logician, they too were determined, and each would have me but a reflection of his own face in a mirror.

"Therefore I came to this place. I find it more sane here. At least, I can be myself."

Then of a sudden, he turned to me and he said, "But tell me, were you also driven to this place by education and good counsel?"

And I answered, "No, I am a visitor."

And he said, "Oh, you are one of those who live in the madhouse on the other side of the wall."

33. We All Are Forerunners

Now that AI (Artificial Intelligence) and robotics have already started replacing human labor, what a boon this must be to us! No longer we have to endure uninteresting works like robots and slaves, and we can start doing inspiring ones with enthusiasm and passion. This is to say that one can engage oneself in creative living.

What kind of life will be a creative one?

Wouldn't it be, to each one's own inclination and longing, to draw and write, to sing and dance, to love, to one's heart's delight?

In other words, wouldn't it be to be a forerunner?

Let's recall as a reminder "The Forerunner" from THE FORERUNNER (1920) by Kahlil Gibran (1883-1931).

THE FORERUNNER

You are your own forerunner, and the towers you have built are but the foundation of your giant-self. And that self too shall be a foundation.

And I too am my own forerunner, for the long shadow stretching before me at sunrise shall gather under my feet at the noon hour. Yet another sunrise shall lay another shadow before me, and that also shall be gathered at another noon.

Always have we been our own forerunners, and always shall we be. And all that we have gathered and shall gather shall be but seeds for fields yet unploughed. We are the fields and the ploughmen, the gatherers and the gathered.

When you were a wandering desire in the mist, I too was there a wandering desire. Then we sought one another, and out of our eagerness dreams were born. And dreams were time limitless, and dreams were space without measure.

And when you were a silent word upon life's quivering lips, I too was there, another silent word. Then life uttered us and we came down the years throbbing with memories of yesterday and with longing for tomorrow, for yesterday was death conquered and tomorrow was birth pursued.

And now we are in God's hands. You are a sun in His right hand and I am an earth in His left hand. Yet you are not more, shining, than I, shone upon.

And we, sun and earth, are but the beginning of a greater sun and a greater earth. And always shall we be the beginning.

You are your own forerunner, you the stranger passing by the gate of my garden.

And I too am my own forerunner, though I sit in the shadows of my trees and seem motionless.

34. May The Jolie Good Era of the Cosmian Age Be Born!

The Hollywood actress Angelina Jolie, the UN special envoy, recently told BBC that she was considering a move into politics, saying she would go where she was needed. She is an active campaigner on a range of issues, including refugees, sexual violence and conservation. In addition to her three biological children, three more children were adopted from orphanages in Cambodia, Ethiopia, and Vietnam, respectively. In 2013, the Hollywood film industry recognized Angelina Jolie with a humanitarian award for her work with refugees and advocating for human rights through her film career. Upon receiving the Jean Hersholt Humanitarian Award, Jolie remembered her late mother who encouraged her to live a life of use to others, although she said it took time for her to realize what that meant.

This is what she said: "I came into this business young and worried about my own pain. And it was only when I began to travel and look and live beyond my home that I began to understand my responsibility to others. When I met survivors of war and famine and rape, I learned what life is like for most people in the world. And how fortunate I was to have food to eat, a roof over my head, a safe place to live, and the joy of having my family safe and healthy. I realized how sheltered I had been, and I was determined never to be that way again.

"We are all, everyone in this room, so fortunate. I have never understood why some people are lucky enough to be born with the chance I had, to have this path in life, and why across the world there's a woman just like me, with the same abilities and the desires, same work ethic and love for her family, who would most likely make better films and better speeches, only she sits in a refugee camp, and she has no voice. She worries about what her children will eat, how to keep them safe, and if they'll ever be allowed to return home. I don't know why this is my life and that's hers.

"I don't understand that, but I will do the best I can with this life to be of use."

When we make her the next U.S. President and the world leader, I pray, she will give birth to The Jolie Good Era of The Cosmian Age!

35. *Funny Stuff*

At the beginning of each year, people exchange greetings, wishing each other a happy new year with many blessings.

What's happiness? Is it something to be found or to be created? If blessings are already there, they should be found. If not, they should be created. Isn't it?

Among blessings, what would be more blissful than fun, laughter, and love?

Let's consider "fun" as a synonym of happiness. If we grown-ups too can enjoy life like children playing house, how much better our world will be!

We can find a role model in Herbert David Kelleher (1931-2019), the co-founder, later CEO, and chairman emeritus of Southwest Airlines until his death on January 3, 2019.

Here are a couple of Herbert Kelleher quotes:

"We have a strategic plan. It's called doing things."

"Think small and act small, and we'll get bigger. Think big and act big, and we'll get smaller."

"A company is stronger if it is bound by love rather than by fear."

"What we are looking for, first and foremost, is a sense of humor," Kelleher—dubbed by Fortune magazine as the "High Priest of Ha—Ha—" has been quoted as saying.

And consequently, it's been recited: "How Fun Flies At Southwest Airlines!"

To cite a couple of in-flight announcements, for example:

"In case you are displeased with our service, there are six exits aboard this aircraft…"

"There is a smoking section, over the wing, or that the movie that was currently playing was, Gone with the Wind."

The fun-loving CEO Herb Kelleher himself dressed up as Elvis Presley or the Easter bunny, just to keep his employees smiling, or settled a business dispute with an arm-wrestling contest.

Wow, how I wish all the disputes between nations could be settled like this between the leaders and how I fancy there would be love-making games in the Olympics instead of the most barbaric, cruel and violent sports called boxing and wrestling. Ha—Ha—

36. *Fate or Destiny?*

If what can be changed is "destiny," "fate" must be what cannot be changed. If destiny is the small picture, fate must be the big frame. If how you happened to be born into a certain species, time and space, in the environmental setting, with your kind of DNA is your fate, then what picture you draw within the frame must be your destiny.

"運命" are the Chinese characters of destiny ("운명" in Korean), "運," the first character of which means "changeable/moveable." "宿命" are the Chinese characters of fate ("숙명" in Korean), "宿," the first character of which means "to sleep over/settled." "命" is the same second Chinese character of both, which means "the breath in the throat/the breath of life."

As for the frame or box we are in, there are two different kinds, so separate from each other. One is factual and real and the other is all made-up and unnatural. They are non-fiction and fiction in literary terms, and reality, virtual reality and augmented reality in computer terms. If our daily lives are the former, all the other arbitrarily and artificially imposed and manipulated ideological thoughts, religious dogma, arts, and literature must be the latter. Like it or not, one has to accept the former as a given. But as to the matter of the latter, one has to decide whether to settle down in the box or get out of the frame, breaking every chain and throwing off all the shackles of slavery.

Let's think of Abraham Lincoln.

Definition of lot in English by Oxford dictionaries is a particular group or set of people or things, an item or set of items, the making of a decision by random selection, especially by a method involving the choice of one from a number of pieces of folded paper, one of which has a concealed mark, a plot of land, or a person's luck, situation, or destiny in life.

Among Lincoln quotes, there's one about "casting one's lot":

"Whatever woman may cast her lot with mine, should any ever do so, it is my intention to do all in my power to make her happy and contented; and there is nothing I can imagine that would make me more unhappy than to fail in the effort."

As we can see these days, a few courageous ladies are turning their "fates" into their "destinies" by joining the current worldwide #MeToo campaign, while the majority of victims are still suffering in the dark, with their fates are being fossilized in caves.

To cite another kind of example, sad to say, some young people choose their careers and even their spouses, dictated by their adulterated parents and societies, instead of carving out their destinies by their own choices.

Anyway, be it the fate or the destiny, if one has to be happy with oneself, after all, it behooves us all to ponder what Lincoln had to say:

"When I do good, I feel good, when I do bad, I feel bad, that's my religion." And this too: "The best way to predict the future is to create it."

37. *Our Nature Is Service*

In the words of the Hungarian writer László Krasznahorkai (b. 1954), winner of the Man Booker International Prize in 2015, spoken in an interview with The Guardian in 2012, "Human existence is worthwhile as a chance to" (if I may paraphrase it) "have some power to say something, for one sentence."

The official citation for the International Booker prize for an "achievement in fiction on the world stage" was:

"What strikes the reader above all are the extraordinary sentences, sentences of incredible lengths, their tone switching from solemn to madcap to quizzical to desolate as they go their wayward way; epic sentences that, like a lint roll, pick up all sorts of odd and unexpected things as they accumulate inexorably into paragraphs that are as monumental as they are scabrous and musical."

Chair of judges Marina Warner said:

"László Krasznahorkai is a visionary writer of extraordinary intensity and vocal range who captures the texture of present-day existence in scenes that are terrifying, strange, appallingly comic, and often shatteringly beautiful. The Melancholy Resistance, Santango, and Seiobo There Below are magnificent works of deep imagination and complex passions, in which the human comedy verges painfully onto transcendence."

The title of the cover story of TIME, February 26, 2018, was:

HOW TO LIVE LONGER, BETTER: You're still going to die, though.

Based on my own experience of having so far lived for 83-odd years, the answer I arrived at is this:

You live as much as you love, for if you don't love, life is meaningless.

I'd like to share this anonymous quote presumed from Native American Indians, who are ethnically related to Koreans:

"The rivers don't drink their own water;
the trees don't eat their own fruits.

The sun doesn't shine for itself;
the flowers don't give their fragrance
to themselves.

To live for others is nature's way---

Life is good when you are happy;
but life is much better when others are happy
because of you!

Who doesn't live to serve,
doesn't deserve to live.
Our nature is service."

Let's recite this little poem by Rumi:

"Come to the orchard in Spring.
There is light and wine, and sweethearts
in the pomegranate flowers.

If you do not come, these do not matter.
If you do come, these do not matter."

38. The Sea of Cosmos

Always changing and impermanent though life is,
Troubled and sorrowful though life is,
What a blessing to be born than not to be born at all!
What felicity to love somebody,
Even if you may be crossed in love and heartbroken!
Aren't all beings born from the Cosmos of Love!

The years passed and I became an old man. I, and my three grandchildren, Elijah, Theodore, and Julia, we were sitting on the shore, looking up at the sky strewn with stardust.

Gazing at the stars, six-year-old Theodore said, "Why don't you ask me where I come from?"

I responded, "Even when you go back, you'll still be in my heart. So it really doesn't matter whether you leave or stay."

"That's true. Do you still miss your Cosmos?" ten-year-old Elijah asked me.

"Of course, everything is the sea of cosmos for me."

After a bit of silence, I continued, "I've grown old now. I'm at the age to compose a poem eulogizing my own death beforehand."

"What's that?" my three-year-old only granddaughter Julia asked with a lovely grimace.

"In actual fact, it's a eulogy to life." The children became very quiet.

I shed tears, thinking aloud, "How much more precious is a moment of human existence than the eternity of divinity meaningless to mortals?" Raising my body, I looked at the night sea. There was the sea of cosmos spread out in front of me. I paused for a moment, then went on to elaborate on the "eulogy to life," while the three children fell asleep, one by one, in my arms, Julia on my lap and Elijah and Theodore at my sides.

The Greek philosopher Epicurus' dictum "carpe diem" epitomizes his philosophy of life. This two-word phrase literally means "to seize the day." It is used to urge someone to make the most of the present time and give little thought to the future; to enjoy the present, as opposed to placing all the hope in the future. It also presents youth as ephemeral and advises the pursuit of pleasure.

"The truth is," I continued, "children are the embodiment of happiness, enjoying life instinctively as the great practitioners of this maxim of Epicurean philosophy. Even their cries are not cries but shrieks of laughter; the cosmic sound of child-song; the ancient music of joy and thankfulness. They are our native symphonic tunes in rhythm with the sea to celebrate our original blessing and our ultimate destination. It's our cosmic chorus: "Star One, Me One; Star Two, Me Two; Star Three, Me Three…" This is the Cosmic Cantata."

The children were fast asleep. There was only the celestial music of all the stars in the wind blowing from the summer sea. Sitting with the children, I saw the stars of the night-sea and had a vision of cosmos flowering everywhere. Looking back on my earlier days, I was amazed at what happened all along. I took a walk down memory lane.

I never married my Cosmos. A bastion of my virginity collapsed unexpectedly. Repulsed by grownups' self-righteous hypocrisy from early on, I posed as a "lamb in wolf's clothing." My crude behavior attracted many girls, but despite my vulgar language, I had always acted like a saint until one fateful night.

As if a monkey falls from a tree by an unforeseen accident under the influence of alcohol, I happened to sleep with a girl without having had a date with her. Feeling morally responsible, I proposed to marry her. But this very smart and independent-minded young lady, to my great surprise, rejected me, saying we didn't have to get married just because we'd had sex. Having always believed that "action speaks louder than words," I decided to go by her action, not by her words and tried hard to persuade her to marry me. To make matters worse, her family put up strong opposition.

Undeterred, and more determined to overcome all adversities, I persevered and two years later we married, but the marriage ended two years after that. Soon after getting a divorce, I learned that she was pregnant with our third child. So I decided to remarry her and to make our marriage work for the sake of the children.

After trying harder for eighteen more years, however, we were divorced for the second time due to our intrinsic and unremitting incompatibility. I learned, the hard way, that you can't change yourself, let alone others. A cat is a cat. It cannot become a dog or vice versa, so to speak. That is to say that one has to like it or not "as is." Perhaps it was a wrong match from the beginning. Had we truly loved each other, we might have been able to transcend all the differences, difficulties, weaknesses and misfortunes.

In retrospect, since early childhood, I had been influenced by the sayings of great people. Brainwashed and hypnotized, I would tell myself that mine was a big fire, unlike a candle's flame or small fire easily extinguished even by a breeze. No, mine was more like an eternal star that comes to shine as soon as the sky is dark enough, or like a kite that rises highest against the wind, not with it. Thus I was never discouraged by anything. On the contrary, I was ever more heartened and inspired, come what may.

Striving desperately for over eighty years, I came to realize, at last, that nothing can be forced against the nature of things. Anything that's meant to happen will happen, and if it is not meant to happen, it never will, no matter what.

And yet, it might be possible to mold oneself one way or another, quite early on, in all probability.

Like Hae-a, everybody living on earth must be protected by one's own guardian angel. Otherwise, how could anyone live through rough times: all the disasters, calamities and catastrophes? One never knows what to expect from one day to the next, as the landscape, seascape, moonscape, and dreamscape are always changing.

If "head-works" were thoughts, "heart-works" might be called arts. From early childhood, I liked songs and enjoyed music, being sentimental and sensitive to everything like all children. When I heard a song, the words fascinated me and I was instantly carried away by the melodies. But was I born tone-deaf? I couldn't sing along with the music. Then what made my three children major in music?

The first thing I did in my married life was to buy a piano, a deluxe stereo system and hundreds of records in an effort to make it up to my wife. Her family almost disowned her for marrying me with no prospects or fortune to inherit. She left her piano at her parents' home, a gift on entering a prestigious girls' middle school in Seoul. The audio system and many records she had bought with her own money, earned as a bank employee after college, were also left behind with her parents. Since she didn't continue to play the piano regularly, it was less functional and more decorative. But after our children were born, the piano became a toy again which she could play with them.

To me, who grew up like a street urchin, the Western classical music was something a child born with a silver spoon in one's mouth could indulge in, just like the upstarts who monopolized playing golf in South Korea after the "Liberation" of Korea from the Japanese at the end of World War II.

When my family moved to England, our children went to a local school in Luton, Bedfordshire. One day, an itinerant music teacher visited the school our oldest child, Hae-a, attended. Pupils interested in learning to play an instrument were given just a ten-minute lesson a week and instruments were loaned to them by the school. Thus began music lessons for our children, one after another, the oldest and the youngest on the violin and the middle one on the cello.

Before long, a few months after they started making all kinds of noise, we had to leave England for Hawaii where their grandma and two aunts lived. Short though it was, they must have enjoyed the lessons enough to practice hard and do well. Their music teachers were sad that they had to leave.

Soon after we arrived in Hawaii, I received a letter inviting our children to return. I was deeply grateful to the music teachers who made arrangements for an audition at the Chetham's School of Music in Manchester, England. No matter how slim a chance it was, I couldn't throw it away. I would rather cast away all the money for the airfares. Although we didn't expect any of our girls to pass the audition, I was not going to deprive them of a thousandth of a one percent chance of success. Much to everyone's surprise, all three passed and were accepted. But it was a very expensive boarding school, way beyond our means. So there was nothing we could do about it. We were just about to go back to Hawaii when the school offered full scholarships to the three little sisters, a godsend undreamed of.

Thus it came to pass that the children left home early, at the ages seven to ten. Had music been forced upon them, they would have feigned interest at first but they would have quit too soon. This seemed to be an example of the effect of one's own inclination. If one likes it, whatever it was, one couldn't help doing it with enthusiasm without even making an effort and it became so much fun.

In the hope that my children would stay young and childlike forever; that they would love everything and not miss a thing, I named them with one common syllable "a" "아" in the Korean alphabet, (meaning "child" in Chinese

105

character "兒") in their first names. Praying they would live on the cosmic energy of the sea, the sky, and the stars, I named them with another Chinese character in each name as Hae-a, 해아, 海兒, meaning the Sea-child; Su-a, 수아, 秀兒, meaning the Sky-child (of excellence); and Song-a, 성아, 星兒, meaning the Star-child. Didn't the American Native Indians go into the woods for a revelation as to what to name themselves? Long may they continue to live up to their names like a long-lasting couple growing to look alike in time. All children are very dear to their parents, but they are infinitely more endearing and sweeter to their grandparents. Everything they do is so amazingly wonderful and heart-achingly precious, to be cherished for eternity.

My youngest daughter, Song-a, displayed her star quality from her early days. Thank her lucky star for its namesake! She did her impressions of celebrities on T.V. and everybody was captivated by her performance. Even before she went to a nursery school, she would shoo away all the boys flocking around her like a swarm of flies. She would do so without uttering a sound. She just gave them a sharp look or the lyric expressions on the face. She would talk down to grown-ups, using more grownup vocabulary. I couldn't admonish her. Every time I tried to do so, I was instantly disarmed. When I yelled at her in a burst of anger, she put me in my place right off by raising her tiny index finger to her pretty lips or whispering in my ear, "You don't have to shout." And I hushed.

At times, she seemed to be a dainty sprite popped out of a myth or a fairy tale. When I appeared to be lecturing her about her homework, she looked me straight in the eye like a child looking at a gorilla behind the bars in a zoo. When I went to the bathroom, she was there right behind me and surprised me peeing. And she asked, "Dad, did you shake?"

My middle one, Su-a, was extraordinary, even as an infant. Was it due to her name? Was she a born rebel? She wouldn't do anything if she were told to do it. If she were told not to do it, she would do it one way or another. Whatever she did, she did as much and when she wanted. That's why people called her "Crazy Super Su-a." Once her interest was awakened, there was no stopping her. When she laughed, she would roll over and over on the floor. Life was a time for play and the world was her playground. This little playgirl never stopped until she had exhausted herself. No wonder she would often fall asleep at the dinner table. She was a fearless adventurer.

After we arrived in England on February 14, 1972, we lived in a rented house in Kings Langley, Hertfordshire. One Sunday morning, I looked into the children's bedroom. The oldest and the youngest were still asleep. But the middle one's bed was empty. I found her downstairs. She was in a complete daze after taking a whole bottle of baby aspirins as if they were candies. Apparently, one-and-a-half-year-old Su-a climbed up a high chair at the breakfast table and took the bottle out of a medicine cabinet in the kitchen. She was rushed to the hospital and her life was saved.

That summer, we were vacationing in Cornwall in S.W. England. We rented a camper on a hill near the beach. While preparing the breakfast one morning, I looked out the window and saw our car, parked next to the camper, was slowly moving down the hill. Even more shocking was a live daredevil stunt action of two-year-old Su-a jumping out of the driver's seat from the rolling car. What if she had been run over by the car? The car crashed into a ditch at the bottom of the hill. She must have climbed into the car and released the handbrake.

At one time when Su-a was three, I came home at the weekend as usual from my weekly business trip. I had a lot to tell my wife. Su-a kept interrupting us and she got a scolding from her mother for not waiting until we finished talking. Still, she didn't stop and tried to engage me in conversation. Beginning to get annoyed with her persistence, I yelled at her to shut up. She didn't even blink. "Dad, now you talk to Mom." She replied, with a nonchalant shrug and left the room.

Su-a always had to have the last word in any argument. She was so quick-witted, most often one or two steps ahead of everybody. When we went shopping, not sure what to buy, we usually asked Su-a for a smart choice. Talking to Su-a, I burst out laughing time and again waving an invisible flag of unconditional surrender, for she had already presented a more convincing counter-argument even before I could make out a case. Soon after her older sister, Hae-a, started on the violin, unbeknownst to her parents Su-a went to Hae-a's violin teacher to ask for a cello teacher, saying she liked the cello sound better. That day, she came home with a quarter-size cello loaned to her by the school. She kept scraping away at the cello for six hours, skipping supper altogether.

Later, after taking a couple of lessons, Su-a followed Hae-a to a rehearsal for the Youth Orchestra concert in the evening. The rest of us arrived at the concert hall in good time. Until the concert started, Su-a didn't come to sit with us. I was beginning to feel nervous and distinctly uneasy about Su-a's whereabouts. The moment I looked at the stage, I was frightened out of my wits and almost fainted. Seven-year-old Su-a was playing in the orchestra, sitting on the edge of a chair with her legs dangling over the sides of her tiny cello among much bigger children, including high school students.

I thought it must be on account of her name. I thought, *too, long may it continue.*

My firstborn Hae-a, her quiet and calm outward appearance notwithstanding, was a child of "inexhaustible" energy and passion, brimming with confidence and courage, her teachers used to remark in her school report cards. Was perception reality? As Hae-a came into being, it was the realization of what I wished, imagined and dreamed. While my wife was expecting twins, I named them Hae-a, 해아, in Korean alphabet meaning "the child of the Sun" and Hae-a, 海兒 in Chinese characters meaning "the child of the sea," as my personal mantra for them to be "sunny" and "romantic." But then they were born premature and put in incubators. One survived and the other one became the surviving twin's guardian angel.

May Hae-a, Su-a, and Song-a and everybody else sojourning on earth have no bad weather, only different kinds of good weather, rain or shine.

I traveled light right back to the future. Many moons ago, when I was working as a houseboy, my two surrogate father figures, one American and the other one British promised to send me to the Juilliard School and to Oxford University; it was not meant to be. Even so, my two children went there instead, Hae-a to Oxford and Su-a to Juilliard.

In September 2013, I wrote "An Open Letter: The Sea of Cosmos," which was sent to U.S. President Obama and Russian President Putin. The Sept. 12, 2013, Op-Ed article in *The New York Times*: "A Plea for Caution From Russia" by Vladimir V. Putin, president of Russia, prompted me to write this letter to all my fellow human beings all over the world.

In concluding his plea, Mr. Putin says that he carefully studied Mr. Obama's address to the nation on Tuesday (September 10, 2013) and that he disagreed about the case President Obama put forth when he stated that the United States' policy is, "What makes America different. It's what makes us [the United States] exceptional."

I, for one, concur with President Putin's apt comment that "It is extremely dangerous to encourage people to see themselves as exceptional, whatever the motivation." From time immemorial, most, if not all, human tragedies have been visited upon us, in my humble opinion, by two major mindsets: One is the self-serving "chosen-species-racist" view, and the other is the harmful concept of "original sin" instilled in childhood.

I firmly believe in the truth that we, not only human beings, but all things in Nature are one and the same. We'd be far better off if we were enlightened early on to realize we are related—part of each other—as the ancient aphorism goes: 피아일체 "pee-ah-il-che" in Korean phonetic alphabet and 彼我一體 in Chinese characters, meaning that "we (you and I) are one and the same." Another aphorism goes 물아일체 "mool-ah-il-che" in Korean phonetic alphabet and "物我一體" in Chinese characters, meaning that "all things and I are one and the same." Simply put, when I hurt or help you, I'm hurting or helping myself; when I destroy or divine Nature, I'm destroying or divining myself. Perhaps that's why and how it's possible that eternity consisted of a flash of a lightning-like moment when we become the very object of our love, as the German mystic Jakob Boehme (1575-1624) believed. Let me further present my case in point. Born in now-North Korea, I happened to be in the south when the country was divided at the end of World War II, which ended the 35-year-old colonial rule of Korea by Japan; hence the Korean War in the heat of the Cold War tension and its ongoing aftermath. By virtue of serendipity and survival instinct of "sink or swim," I've always counted every stroke of luck as a blessing and believed nothing is to be discarded.

Eleventh of 12 children, I became fatherless at the age of five and homeless when I was thirteen during the Korean War. Consequently, I went on a journey at an early age, in search of the sublime in our human condition, seeking my cosmic identity in the greater scheme of things. No matter where one is from, if we look at things from the big picture, we all are "cosmians arainbow" passing through as fleeting sojourners on this tiny leaf-boat-like planet earth floating in the sea of cosmos.

If each one of us, be it a grain of sand, a drop of water, a blade of grass, or a human being, is indeed a micro-cosmos reflecting a macro-cosmos of all that existed in the past, all that exists in the present and all that will exist in the future, we're all in it together, all on our separate journeys to realize we must all sing the Cosmos Cantata together. No one is exceptional and all of us are exceptional.

When I was diagnosed with prostate cancer fourteen years ago, I started to compose a short, true story of my life in the form of a fairy tale for my five daughters as my only legacy. All I wanted to say in my writings is this:

> *Always changing and impermanent though life is,*
> *Troubled and sorrowful though life is,*
> *What a blessing it is to be born than not to be born at all!*
> *What felicity it is to love somebody,*
> *Even if you may be crossed in love and heart-broken!*
> *Isn't it such a beautiful, blissful and wonderful experience?*
> *To live and to love!*
> *By so doing we learn to fly and to soar.*

And a small portion of my daughter's recent eulogy to her husband reflects those sentiments:

> *I spoke of how ridiculously lucky I felt to have met him.*
> *How I had no regrets about anything on our journey.*
> *I told him that I had never sought for perfection in anything in my life.*
> *But that somehow, I had found it.*

I had found it in "us."
We were perfect.
Perfect in our imperfections too.
Our imperfectly perfect balance.

And Doris Wenzel, the American publisher of my book *Cosmos Cantata* reflected on their exceptional lives in:

To The Couple I Do Not Know

I have never met those two young people,
Impressing those who know them,
Inspiring those who don't.

I have never met those two young lovers,
Wrapped in devotion to one another,
Celebrating life alone and with others.

I have never met those two sweet souls,
Securing a world of their own
While creating a lingering melody for the world.

After I learned of his (Gordon's) passing at the age of 46, I emailed the following short message to my daughter:

Dearest Su-a,
It is good to know that Gordon listened and understood what you had to say for an "eternal" hour before he stopped breathing and he was gone so "peacefully."
Su-a, you are such an amazing girl. I'm even envious of you, not only for having found "the love of your life" but

113

more for living it to the best, to the fullest, so intensely, so poetically, very short though it was only for 13 months.

Even if one lives to be over a hundred, still it will be nothing but a breath, a droplet of waves breaking on the shore, returning to the sea of cosmos. Thus we never leave "the sea inside."

Love, Dad XX

39. Doing One's Best

(Originally published in THE KOREA TIMES, Thursday, November 8, 1979.)

When I came home after leaving my young children aged seven to ten at a boarding school of music in Manchester, England, I wrote to them as follows:

My Dearest Hae-a, Su-a and Song-a,

You might not be so happy for the moment and I am worried a bit. But I am quite sure that you will be well settled in the new environment and will soon be as happy as you make your minds to be. Don't let all the challenges frighten you away. Be brave and meet the challenges with courage and confidence. I know you will. Remember that "kites rise highest against the wind, not with it; that in everything bitter, there is buried something sweet; and that the journey of a thousand miles begins with one pace." So laugh your fears away and you will certainly have the last laugh.

It is not so much how you start as how you end; it is not so much how far you go as what you see; it is not so much how much you see as what you learn from what you see; it is not so much how much you learn as what you do with what you learn from what you see as you go wherever you plan to go, as a teacher's saying goes.

Just simply try to do what seems best for you each day, as each day comes. Give yourselves completely now to what you are doing. Don't baby yourselves. Set up for yourselves a goal of excellence and set a high standard for yourselves.

If you get behind, concentrate totally and completely because one of the great thrills is to come from behind and win. Don't be a quitter. If you get beat, try all the harder next time. But don't ever quit when you are behind.

How you think determines what you achieve. Try to get your thinking right before every practice or lessons. For a moment, close your eyes. Your prayers should be that of thanks to those who made it possible for you to be there at Chatham's. Think of how lucky and fortunate you are and make sure that you don't waste the wonderful opportunities given to you. Then, end with a prayer of joy for competition. For, competition is the very substance of life. It is the molding and testing process where you have your chance to express the very best that is in you. Mind you, you are not competing with anybody but with yourselves, that is, to reach and to realize your full potential.

The evergreen pines you saw in Korea are born to wind and sleet, and live a long, long time, thanks to their tough core and clinging roots. The stately royal palms you saw in Hawaii are nurtured in warm sun and tropic breezes. Their pith is soft. Their roots are shallow. They can't survive the hurricane. Durable are the children who have been taught to love the storm.

Always remember and never forget that you are children of the Sea, the Sky and the Star, and that you are to swim in the sea of love, to sail in the sky of hope and to grow into three brilliant stars of celestial music.

You know how to make your dreams come true. Don't you? Make the best of what you have. Don't waste time, above all. Time is the most precious thing, for it passes quickly, as you know. Once the moments, the hours and days pass, they are gone forever. Never the same moments, hours and days do return, like a running brook that sings its melody with no repeat to eternity.

You alone can build your own future. Your tomorrows depend on what you do with your todays. Your future will be what you build at present. Like the farmer, as you sow, so you shall reap. You can get only what you put in. Nothing will be gained from outside, unless and until you get ready and prepared within.

You alone can change your own pattern. By changing the inner attitudes of your minds, you can change the outer aspects of your lives. You can change either for the better or for the worse. History and literature are full of examples of the miracle of inner change. I wonder if you remember the Persian story of the hunchback princess who became straight and tall, by standing each day before a statue of herself made straight. Let go of lower things and reach for the higher. Surround yourselves with the very best in friends, books, music, and art. Try to improve yourselves all the time.

Whatever you do, try to do it as well as you can, as excellently as you can. The hard fact that we can never be perfect leaves limitless room for improvement. There is no

117

limit to your progress. Like the phrase, literally, "The sky is the limit!" Exciting, isn't it? (No wonder, as a Hollywood Studio Musician/Violinist and a helicopter pilot, Song-a, you are flying to your gigs, almost like in a fairy tale, ha—ha—.)

When you play the game of darts, if you miss the mark, you turn and look for the fault within yourself. Failure to hit the target's center is never the fault of the target. To improve your aim, you have to improve yourself. Before trying to improve others, try to perfect yourself first.

Once you have done your best, however, nothing should bother you, nothing should worry you, neither failure nor success, neither fortune nor misfortune. You can content yourselves with doing your very best, be the outcome what it may. Just try to live every moment to the fullest and to live a full life every second. By doing so, you will be able to fulfill yourselves to the utmost.

We are being apart with hundreds of miles between us, missing each other. But let us remember that where there is loneliness, there also is love, and where there is suffering, there also is joy. Being lonely can bring us together more closely and enable us to find ourselves as other-selves of each other, living in each other as part of the whole of us. Through loneliness, we come to realize that we even breathe for each other, radiating love and touching what is most important in each of us. Let us believe that to live is to grow in love and to love is to grow in loneliness, for loneliness keeps open the doors to an expanding life, a greater and happier self, related to the whole of the universe.

My heavenly children of cosmos, enjoy the very best of yourselves, doing your very best at all times to make as beautiful a sound of music as you can out of your hearts and souls, not from your instruments but through them, until you come home in a few weeks' time.

Love from Daddy

(As I wrote this letter, I wondered aloud if what I wrote rings true to myself, let alone to the children.)

* * *

December 30th, 2016

Dearest Dad,

I'm so glad this was published just in time for your 80th birthday!

I hope that you will enjoy reading my chapter on value… you feature quite a lot—and I'm truly grateful for everything that you are, and all the values you have taught me. You are the true reason that I am what I am today.

Huge love,
Su-a

The following was originally published in 2016 by lulu.com. It was Su-a's contribution to a collection of essays entitled "Speaking of Values" compiled by Emma Fossey, Director of Reporting for Business; Neil McLennan, a speaker, author, former education manager, and Director of Leadership Programs of the University of Aberdeen; and Gary Walsh, an education consultant, freelance facilitator, project manager, and researcher.

Our values provide the backbone to our lives. If we didn't have values, we couldn't make sensible progress or have much stability.

I think of values as a system of setting our personal boundaries: like creating our own set of principles that lets us know how far we can go and what is morally acceptable. Much of this comes from family.

I have two sisters and we are very close in age (all three of us within two years and eleven months). We emigrated from South Korea to the UK when we were all babies. My father was away from home for work between Monday and Friday, and only home for weekends. My mother was, therefore, mostly alone with three very young children to look after, in a country that was completely foreign in terms of culture, language and pretty much everything. She had no friends or family to turn to for advice or backup. Even running out of milk was difficult. If there had only been two of us, she could have tucked one under each arm and carried us to the local shop, but because there were three of us, that was not an option. The necessity for some element of control meant that our parents were quite strict.

I vividly remember one early boundary of obedience being set. We were very excited about acquiring our first TV. It was a small square set with coat-hanger antennae sticking out of the back of it, which used to sit on top of a cardboard box. The three of us would love to lie on our stomachs as close as possible to it. This particular weekend, my Dad called us for dinner and got progressively frustrated when we ignored him completely. By the third time of asking, he threatened us, "If you don't join us for dinner now, I am throwing the TV out!" We still didn't move, and true to his word, the TV was duly thrown out! We never replaced the TV and I never had one since.

We also learned how to give and take from an early age. My mother often retells a story about a time when my sisters and I were fighting over a toy. My mother said to us, "If you can't settle this peacefully and learn to share, then none of you gets it!" This must have struck a chord with me because I immediately responded by saying, "It's fine. Song-a (my little sister) can have it. I will have it afterward." Early lessons in the benefit of sharing.

I remember these moments as experiences that taught us a kind of obedience, but we also learned that once the goalposts were set by our parents, they wouldn't move. I feel that without a clear sense of boundaries being set for young people, life can get very confusing. I suppose that these boundaries help us to create our values and this starts from a really early stage. While it is true that there are many more grey areas of "good and bad" for adults, when you are a child it's a bit more black and white. I feel that it is important and helpful for children to have clarity about what is acceptable and what is not; a clear sense of definition that can be a source of guidance. I feel lucky that I grew up with a fairly clear sense of boundaries, instilled by my parents.

Instinct, independence, passion

I am not a very good forward planner. I've never made New Year's resolutions. I make a lot of decisions based on how it feels at that particular moment, as the future is unknowable. If I need to make a choice, often it isn't so much about good or bad but more about how each decision will feel afterward and whether it's "safe to be bold." My decisions and values are very instinctive; some of them might be based on feelings of fear or danger, but I can rationalize them in the moment due to feeling pretty grounded in myself. I am often motivated by my desire to make a group of people happy and I tend to think of this bigger picture.

As a teenager, I was very much aware of rules. I understood the need to have them in place but felt that I could break them if I did so responsibly and for the right reasons. Some of this desire for independence and freedom comes from my time at Chetham's Music School, a specialist music boarding school right in Manchester's city center. My sisters and I all studied there.

At "Chet's" I made my own rules. I didn't break the school rules to be naughty or anti-establishment. I just wanted to feel autonomous and free. Sometimes, for instance, when living in a boarding house was too much for me, I would borrow camping equipment from the school and go off on my own. I would take the train and stay overnight in the countryside, in places like Edale in the Peak District, for example. Of course, it was totally ridiculous, but I didn't feel like I was doing anything very "bad." I just wanted some freedom and to do something on my own. I also knew that I'd never get permission to do such things but that they were good for my soul. I still have that need for freedom today.

I was initially given a violin to play because my older sister was playing one, but to be honest, I hated it. I couldn't hold the weight of it, it hurt my arms and it was an utterly horrid sound and experience! However, after a couple of weeks, I heard a piece on the radio (it was "The Swan") played on the cello, and immediately, I said I wanted to play that. Luckily, the brother of our violin teacher, Derek Williams, was an amateur cellist, Viv Williams, and he agreed to teach me. The only cello available to me was borrowed from a school, and I could only use it on a Saturday morning when Derek ran a string group. I would scrape away there, then be whisked out for twenty minutes to have individual time with Viv. I was much smaller than average for an eight-year-old and the cello was a particularly huge instrument for me, but I instantly fell in love with it. I wasn't allowed to take it home during term time, but I remember the first time I was allowed to take it home for a week's school holiday…it was epic! That first day, I played away at this huge cello for six hours, refusing to come to the table even for dinner because I was a seven-year-old in love. Luckily my dad didn't throw this object out!

I've come to the conclusion that if you love doing something, you will do it without effort. I have had the question about "talent" put to me many times. Is somebody born talented or does it develop? I believe that anybody can learn to play an instrument, I really do. I don't think that people are necessarily born with a talent to play a particular instrument. For me, it comes down to whether you love it enough to be patient with it. I think you can learn most things, such as hearing music effectively, if you really want to. To have a sense of fine-tuning, you need to have the desire, stamina, and patience to do it. I remember struggling to play things in tune, trying to find whole and half tone intervals and then discovering the myriad possibilities even within the half tone. It really was a training of the ear, not just of the fingers. I am still thinking about this now, especially with the different tuning of ethnic cultures around the world.

Taking an interest to the "nth" degree only happens if you are passionate about and love what you are doing. There has to be some kind of emotional connection to ensure that you keep going. If I didn't completely love it, I am sure I would have given up out of sheer frustration. Some people might be able to persevere because of a desire to make a "success" of it, but it's different for me.

I sometimes feel that the education system, particularly the way we train musicians, encourages people more towards notions of success and perfection, and I don't necessarily believe in that. I can identify with musicians who tell stories about being "sick with fear." My sister, for instance, had a panic attack, hyperventilated and dropped her bow in her final recital at Oxford University. She immediately developed a small and contained area of vitiligo on that bowing arm which she still has to this day. We all have the propensity to feel that fear, but I think it is the role of the education system to prevent that from happening, to boost self-confidence and to foster a continued love of what you are doing.

The only time I remember questioning my future in music was when I was sixteen and faced with the decision of planning what to do after school. To be honest, all I wanted to do was play the cello but at that stage, I began to wonder, "What if I can't do this? What if I chopped my finger off or had an accident that prevented me from doing it?" The only other thing that I was passionate about at that time was cooking. During school holidays, I would cook and experiment every day with vegetarian food for my whole (non-vegetarian) family. While I would have always wanted music to play a part in my life, I thought for a while about becoming a chef. I dreamed about opening a vegetarian cafe in Paris that offered live chamber music, as Paris in the '80s was fairly barren for vegetarians.

I still love cooking but I think that I would have found it very stressful because of the need to "perform," and I didn't necessarily want to cook every meal for every day of my life at a consistently high level under pressure.

The same stress is also relevant for musicians, but being part of an orchestra has the advantage of being very much a collective performance and there is a lot of energy from your colleagues to maintain that consistency and drive.

Friendship, community spirit, connecting with people and the next generation

Unlike some of my colleagues who have said that they were ostracized through learning music as a child, I never found this to be the case. There may be reasons for this: first, I was playing to around Grade 6 standard after a year so had progressed quite quickly (as had my violin-playing sisters); second, my family emigrated to Hawaii within a few months of my playing because of my father's job situation; and third, our teachers, Derek and Viv, had an uncle who taught history at Chet's, which is how we became aware of the school's existence. Viv's wife Frankie, who is a force of nature, persuaded my parents to bring us back to England after six months to audition for Chet's. Frankie accompanied us to Manchester, my sisters and I making a secret pact that if one of us didn't get in then none of us would go. But we all got places, and Frankie secured full scholarships for us all through the Leverhulme Trust.

So, I think that thanks to a combination of traveling, fairly fast progress on the cello, and very shortly afterward going to a specialist music boarding school where all my friends were musicians, I didn't have time to feel ostracized.

Because I lived in a small community from a young age—I had just turned nine when I went to Chet's—I think I have a strong sense of what feels good and bad for me as well as for those around me. At school, we had to deal with many social behaviors: some good, some bad. The good side was nurturing, fun, creative, and supportive. The bad side was frightening and I witnessed bullying, fighting, and personality clashes. As a result, throughout my life, I always want every situation to be a good one for everybody involved. If you are not happy as a group of performers, you are not going to play your best. You can't play together if you are not literally and metaphorically on the same page.

This can be difficult to manage sometimes, particularly in small chamber groups where the relationships are particularly intense. Because of the nature of what we do, our radars are overly active and alert, and therefore very like to overreact! In an orchestra, everybody knows each other intimately; you can often predict how people are going to respond and must be prepared for them to be irrational!

Musicians would not be in the business if we didn't have an audience, and music wouldn't have a future if we didn't engage with the next generation. These are huge motivators. I grew up in the youth orchestra system, which is such a great experience. Joining a youth orchestra is like having a whole new world open up and discovering a new way of engaging with people. This engagement gives us so much new material for our developmental progress.

As well as being completely terrifying for all sorts of reasons, it is so much fun. I remember going to see my older sister, Hae-a, playing in our county youth orchestra for the first time. I worried my parents because I had gone backstage with Frankie during the interval and hadn't reappeared for the second half. Imagine their astonishment when they noticed on stage, at the back of the cello section, a tiny pair of dangling legs that could only have been mine. I had wanted to join in the fun. That was my first experience of playing in the youth orchestra. I then progressed through the four Bedfordshire County Youth Orchestras as well as the National Children's Orchestra.

I started coaching youth orchestras myself when I was nineteen. Since then, they have been a constant thread throughout my career, being involved as I have been in youth orchestras all over the UK. While I was studying at the Juilliard School in New York, I was involved in coaching the Iceland Youth Orchestra. We got together three times a year, for a fortnight course each time, for a period of three years. We took on some hefty programs as there was lots of time for thorough sectional coaching, and although they might start barely being able to play the notes, by the end they sounded like a professional orchestra. There was no time pressure, and we got the chance to really bond.

Aged nineteen myself, I wasn't that much older than most of them so that probably helped.

For most young people taking part, it is their first real experience of "community spirit." I remember how that felt for me when I started. The skills you build in a youth orchestra, having to be aware of the people around you and appreciating the fact that it's not all about your own part, are valuable social skills for life. As a coach, for instance, I will often give practical advice to young people on how to be a good desk partner—helping each other to write notes on the music, how to turn pages while performing, organizing the height of the music stand, giving each other enough space and so on. There are so many ways to help each other.

Having gone through the youth orchestra system myself, it is such a privilege to support the next generation to do the same. When I am coaching, I want the process to be fun but disciplined. I can be quite strict, but only in a musical way and it is always fun. That is the balance I strive to achieve as a coach.

This attitude also affects the work I do in my job in the orchestra. On the concert platform, we have moved away from wearing formal concert dress such as tails, but I think we could go much further. Connecting with the audience is incredibly important, and I feel there is so much that we can do and that I can learn from my experiences with young people to help achieve that. This connection is sometimes as simple as chatting to people after a concert or just showing an interest. I am a "people person" in many ways. People are my religion, so to speak, in that they are what I believe in. I am intrigued to find out why people have come to a particular event or what their experience with music has been. Audience members will often come to me after a performance to share how much they enjoyed the event or how it made them feel. Some even tell me that they come just to see what color my hair is! So I feel that, on whatever level, there is a genuine personal connection with audiences.

I know that it makes a difference in people's lives. Once an elderly gentleman in Aberdeen came to me after a Subscriber's Concert, which is a special chamber concert that we invite regular subscribers to, free, as a loyalty bonus. He had attended the concert and was quite emotional. He gave me a gift of a necklace that had belonged to his wife, who had always come particularly to see me play. She had sadly passed away. This is connection on a very deep level and I was overwhelmed by the beauty and bravery of the gesture. These personal connections make the whole experience richer because you know that people are enjoying it and feel connected to it. In the moment of performance, I am not necessarily thinking about the audience—I am focused on the music—but it certainly makes a difference to have that level of feedback and connection with the people around you.

During the past twenty years, alongside my life as an orchestral cellist, I have been incredibly lucky also to have an alternative musical outlet for connecting with audiences and artists from across the musical divides. This is through our band Mr. McFall's Chamber, of which I am a founding member. It started in 1996 as a renegade splinter group from the SCO, presenting classical music to the midnight, underground nightclub scene. Our mission was to experiment, collaborate and break down barriers. In terms of broadening horizons, building bridges with other art disciplines, creating new worlds and exploring other cultures, this band has meant a huge amount to me. We took some of the first steps towards bringing together folk, jazz, and world musicians, as well as dancers, poets, and visual artists. It has allowed freedom of expression and the possibility to grow as an artist and a human being, and I believe we have slowly brought about a big change in the musical landscape of Scotland.

Conclusion

It has been illuminating for me to write this chapter because it has clarified many previously unexplored thoughts about how we shape our individual value systems. It is very clear to me that this process starts when we are extremely young and builds continuously on the ever-growing accumulation of experiences, like choosing which building blocks to use and deciding what shape of construction you want to build. Education and structure, as opposed to training and strictness, are absolutely paramount in this.

I feel very lucky having such inspirational parents, but not everyone is so fortunate. This is where I think the roles of education and its aficionados are so important. The school arena is where all children can experience community outside of the family and all the extremes of human nature that this presents. Of course, this is not limited to just school institutions but extends to other educational or cultural communities. Experiencing these extremes in a safe environment is the best way to discover personal boundaries in a productive way.

Educational communities are also the best nurturing ground for sparking passions. Young children are naturally inquisitive because everything is new to them. It is vital that their developing passions are encouraged and that every child is made to feel confident and independent. This self-confidence and self-determination will give them the bravery to achieve whatever they wish to pour their hearts into.

I would like to conclude with an amusing anecdote. It is from my very first time coaching the Iceland Youth Orchestra and illustrates how travel, music, creativity, and fun all contribute to what can happen when you connect with people.

I arrived in Iceland on Boxing Day at the crack of dawn (although that's a misnomer since, at that time of year, the sun never rises in Iceland!). I was being hosted by a family of five, whose eighteen-year-old daughter was playing violin in the youth orchestra. There was also a twelve-year-old daughter and a five-year-old son.

Having apologized for getting them out of bed so early on Boxing Day, I tried to explain to the mother that I was a vegetarian and therefore didn't eat meat or fish. I hastened to add that I didn't want to inconvenience them by expecting them to cook expensive vegetables, so I said I would just eat what they ate but that because it was not my normal fare, I hoped for their understanding. The mother, with a wicked glint in her eye, took this as the go-ahead to try to tempt me with all their Icelandic specialties, such as raw, rotten shark (which is buried underground as part of the preparation process), seared sheep's head with eyes and tongue gouged out, blood pudding and puffin! I was most definitely not compliant!

When it became clear that on New Year's Day they would prepare me a "special meal," I was dreading it. When the time came, I was almost trembling, seeing their palpable excitement. They dimmed the lights and wheeled in the meal on a trolley. It had one of these huge silver butler cloches on it. They asked me, as their guest of honor, to present it. After a long, deep breath I whipped off the cloche and then screamed my (own) head off! What I had revealed staring up at me, was the head of their twelve-year-old daughter on the platter, surrounded by vegetables!

After my initial terror, I found it monstrously funny. They enjoyed telling me how they had even cut a hole in their sideboard to perform this wicked practical joke. I am still in touch with the family and I see them regularly even today.

Music knows no boundaries; it simply brings people together.

Korean born cellist Su-a Lee is one of the highlights of the Scottish music scene. Feted wherever she goes, she stands out for her versatility, popularity, and appetite for musical adventure. Born in Seoul, Su-a trained at Chetham's School of Music, completing her studies at the Juilliard School in New York. On graduating with her degree, she moved to Scotland to join the Scottish Chamber Orchestra, where she remains as Assistant Principal Cello. While she is deeply rooted in her Scottish home, Su-a and her cello have appeared all over the world, from South

America to Arctic Circle. As well as performing in the world's major concert halls, you are just as likely to find them in such unorthodox and interesting locations as Japanese temples, circus tents, and waterfalls.

Although Su-a spends most of her time playing classical music, she is very much in demand across a wide musical spectrum, working in all art forms. She has played for theatre, dance and film projects, and performs and records regularly with Scotland's jazz and folk stars. Over the summer 2015, she spent six months studying and collaborating with musicians from across the globe, incorporating genres of folk, classical, Arabic, Celtic, Swedish and Eastern traditions. Her non-classical work has included recording on her Musical Saw for Eric Clapton and performing at Celtic Connections with Jack Bruce of Cream and the folk band Lau, to improvisatory work with the Belgian theatre group Reckless Sleepers and a tour of India with the Sarod maestro, Amjad Ali Khan.

Su-a is also a founder member of the innovative music ensemble, Mr. McFall's Chamber. Beginning in 1996 playing avant-garde string quartet music in late-night club venues, the group has just celebrated its 20th anniversary season and has grown to encompass an eclectic range of different traditions.

With a special passion for working with young musicians, Su-a regularly participates in SCO Connects education and community work, and recently toured a very successful series of performances for babies with Reeling and Writhing Theatre. She is Patron-in-Chief of the Perth Youth Orchestra, a regular coach for the National Youth Orchestra and Cambridge County Youth Orchestra. She is an Associate Member of the Martyn Bennett Trust and a Trustee for the Board of the Soundhouse Trust.

40. How to Be Free
in Body and Soul

Now we are entering a new kind of New Age. It started in the auto industry since 2017. It is called a "subscription economy." In place of all the hassles and headaches for purchasing or leasing, insurance, license, maintenance, tax, etc., you just pay a subscription fee to a service company that takes care of everything for you, while you pick and choose what model of a car you want whenever you need it. Imagine this trend spreading into other industries, say dating, education, entertainment, housing, restaurant, and travel businesses. What a free lifestyle to be detached from it all in body and soul! After all, aren't we all are wanderers? Nevertheless, we are reminded that there's THE OTHER WANDERER in "The Wanderer: His Parables and Sayings" (1932) by Kahlil Gibran (1883-1931).

THE OTHER WANDERER

Once on a time I met another man of the roads. He too was a little mad, and thus he spoke to me:

"I am a wanderer. Oftentimes it seems that I walk the earth among pygmies. And because my head is seventy cubits farther from the earth than theirs, it creates higher and freer thoughts.

"But in truth I walk not among men but above them, and all they can see of me is my footprints in their open fields.

"And often have I heard them discuss and disagree over the shape and size of my footprints. For there are some who say, 'These are the tracks of a mammoth that roamed the earth in the far past.' And others say, 'Nay, these are places where meteors have fallen from the distant stars.'

"But you, my friend, you know full well that they are naught save the footprints of a wanderer."

41. *"Love Myself"*

(On September 24, 2018, all seven members of the K-pop group took the floor as UNICEF's goodwill ambassadors, and its group BTS leader RM, born Kim Nam-joon addressed the United Nations floor in support of the launch of "Youth 2030: The United Nations Youth Strategy" along with the "Generation Unlimited Partnership." The goals of these programs are to listen to the voices of the world's 1.8 billion youth and, by creating innovative programs, to get them in school or age-appropriate work by 2030.)

"It's an incredible honor to be invited to an occasion of such significance for today's young generation. Last November, BTS launched the LOVE MYSELF campaign with UNICEF building on our belief that true love first begins with loving myself. We have been partnering with UNICEF's end violence program to protect children and young people all over the world from violence. And, our fans have become a major part of this campaign with their action and their enthusiasm. We truly have the best fans in the world.

I'd like to begin by talking about myself. I was born in Ilsan, a city near Seoul, South Korea. It is a really beautiful place with a lake, hills, and even an annual flower festival. I spent a very happy childhood there and I was judged like an ordinary boy. I used to look up at the night sky and I used to dream the dreams of a boy. I used to imagine that I was a superhero who could save the world.

In an intro to one of our early albums, there's a line that says, "My heart stopped when I was maybe nine or ten." Looking back, I think that's when I began to worry about what other people thought of me and started seeing myself in their eyes. I stopped looking up at the night skies, the stars. I stopped daydreaming. Instead, I just tried to jam myself into the molds that other people made. Soon, I began to shut out my own voice and started to listen to the voices of others. No one called out my name and neither did I. My heart stopped and my eyes closed shut.

And so, like this I, we, all lost our names. We became like ghosts. But I had one thing and that was music. There was a small voice inside of me that said, "Wake up, man, and listen to yourself." But, it took me quite a long time to hear music calling my real name. Even after making the decision to join BTS, there were a lot of hurdles. Some people might not believe it, but most people thought we were hopeless. And, sometimes, I just wanted to quit. But I think I was very lucky that I didn't give it all up. And, I'm sure that I and we will keep stumbling and falling like this.

BTS has become artists performing in those huge stadiums, and we're selling millions of albums right now. But I am still an ordinary 24-year-old guy. If there's anything that I've achieved, it was only possible that I have my other BTS members right by my side, and because of the love and support that our ARMY fans all over the world made for us. And, maybe I made a mistake yesterday. But, yesterday's me is still me. Today, I am who I am with all of my faults and my mistakes. Tomorrow, I might be a tiny bit wiser, and that would be me too. These faults and mistakes are what I am, making up the brightest stars in the constellation of my life.

I have come to love myself for who I am, for who I was, and for who I hope to become.

I would like to say one last thing. After releasing our "Love Yourself" albums, and launching the Love Myself campaign, we started to hear remarkable stories from our fans all over the world—how our message helped them overcome their hardships in life and to start loving themselves. Those stories constantly remind us of our responsibility. So, let's all take one more step. We have learned to love ourselves, so now I urge you to speak yourself.

I would like to ask all of you, "What is your name?" What excites you and makes your heartbeat? Tell me your story. I want to hear your voice. I want to hear your conviction—no matter who you are or where you're from, your skin color, your gender identity. Just speak yourself. Find your name and find your voice by speaking yourself.

I'm Kim Nam-joon and also RM of BTS. I am an idol and I am an artist from a small town in Korea. Like most people, I've made many mistakes in my life. I have many faults and I have many more fears, but I am going to embrace myself as hard as I can. And, I am starting to love myself gradually, little by little.

"What is your name?"

This speech recalls a quote from C.S. Lewis' "Mere Christianity," published in 1952:

"For a long time, I used to think this a silly, straw-splitting distinction: how could you hate what a man did, and not hate the man? But years later, it occurred to me that there was one man to whom I had been doing this all my life—namely myself. However much I might dislike my own cowardice or conceit or greed, I went on loving myself. Just because I loved myself, I was sorry to find that I was the sort of man who did those things."

It should go without saying that one cannot love and respect others unless and until one can love and respect oneself, and that it's far better to love oneself believing in the original blessing than to hate oneself believing in the "original sin."

Furthermore, how much better to be born incomplete, imperfect, uncharted and unmolded, given carte blanche! Bravo! Cheers!"

42. Cosmian Vision Is the Key

Are Koreans geniuses in concocting trendy catchphrases? They are like "TWIWOL" ("트인낭" in Korean), initials for "Twitting Is Waste Of Life," and "KAFAIN depression" ("카페인 우울증" in Korean), for Kakao (the operator of Korea's dominant mobile messaging app Kakao Talk), Facebook and Instagram depression. Many SNS users are reportedly becoming addicts and ending up depressed.

This must be a reflection of the reality we are experiencing these days. The number of Twitter followers of Trump, the embodiment (to some, if not most, people) of abnormality, absurdity, untruth is said to be in the 57,300,000s and his supporters are to be 30% to 40% of U.S. voters.

One may recite this cry along with THE MADMAN: His Parables and poems (1918) by Kahlil Gibran (1883-1931):

"THE PERFECT WORLD"

GOD of lost souls, thou who art lost amongst the gods, hear me:

Gentle Destiny that watches over us, mad, wandering spirits, hear me:

I dwell in the midst of a perfect race, I the most imperfect.

I, a human chaos, a nebula of confused elements, I move amongst finished worlds—peoples of complete laws and pure order, whose thoughts are assorted, whose dreams are arranged, and whose visions are enrolled and registered.

Their virtues, O God, are measured, their sins are weighed, and even the countless things that pass in the dim twilight of neither sin nor virtue are recorded and catalogued.

Here days and nights are divided into seasons of conduct and governed by rules of blameless accuracy.

To eat, to drink, to sleep, to cover one's nudity, and then to be weary in due time.

To work, to play, to sing, to dance, and then to lie still when the clock strikes the hour.

To think thus, to feel thus much, and then to cease thinking and feeling when a certain star rises above yonder horizon.

To rob a neighbor with a smile, to bestow gifts with a graceful wave of the hand, to praise prudently, to blame cautiously, to destroy a soul with a word, to burn a body with a breath, and then to wash the hands when the day's work is done.

To love according to an established order, to entertain one's best self in a preconceived manner, to worship the gods becomingly, to intrigue the devils artfully—and then forget all as though memory were dead.

To fancy with a motive, to contemplate with consideration, to be happy sweetly, to suffer nobly—and then to empty the cup so that tomorrow may fill it again.

All these things, O God, are conceived with forethought, born with determination, nursed with exactness, governed by rules, directed by reason, and then slain and buried after a prescribed method. And even their silent graves that lie within the human soul are marked and numbered.

It is a perfect world, a world of consummate excellence, a world of supreme wonders, the ripest fruit in God's garden, the master-thought of the universe.

But why should I be here, O God, I a green seed of unfulfilled passion, a mad tempest that seeketh neither east nor west, a bewildered fragment from a burnt planet?

Why am I here, O God of lost souls, thou who art lost amongst the gods?

Nevertheless, crying and wailing over the reality we are facing will be so futile.

Since there's no answer to our questions, we've got to answer them ourselves.

Even though ours is not "the perfect world," we are born with the perfect key to turn our chaotic world into Cosmos. The key is none other than one's Cosmian Vision of Love Arainbow.

43. As I Walk with Beauty

According to Wikipedia, a mirror neuron is a neuron that fires both when an animal acts and when the animal observes the same action performed by another. Thus, the neuron "mirrors" the behavior of the other, as though the observer were itself acting. Such neurons have been directly observed in primate species.

Neuroscientist Giacomo Rizzolatti, MD, who in the 1980s and 1990s with his colleagues at the University of Parma first identified mirror neurons, says that the neurons could help explain how and why we "read" other people's minds and feel empathy for them. If watching an action and performing that action can activate the same parts of the brain in monkeys—down to a single neuron—then it makes sense that watching an action and performing an action could also elicit the same feelings in people.

No doubt all children do it all the time instinctively by nature.

Here are a couple of quotes from Black Elk (1863-1950), the American Native Indian Oglala Lakota (Sioux) leader:

Grown men may learn from very little children, for the hearts of little children are pure, and therefore, the Great Spirit may show to them many things which older people miss. The first peace, which is the most important, is that which comes within the souls of people when they realize their relationship, their oneness, with the universe and all its powers, and when they realize that at the center of the universe dwells Wakan-Tanka, and that this center is really everywhere, it is within each of us.

Describing a childhood vision he had while very ill and near death, Black Elk says:

Then I was standing on the highest mountain of them all, and round about beneath me was the whole hoop of the world. And while I stood there, I saw more than I can tell and I understood more than I saw; for I was seeing in a sacred manner the shapes of all things in the spirit, and the shape of all shapes as they must live together like one being.

Excerpted from Black Elk: Earth Prayer and The Sunset
Thus may it be with us all mirror neurons as twinkling Cosmian starlets!

As I Walk with Beauty ~ A Traditional Navajo Prayer

As I walk, as I walk
The universe is walking with me
In beauty it walks before me
In beauty it walks behind me
In beauty it walks below me

In beauty it walks above me
Beauty is on every side
As I walk, I walk with Beauty.

44. The Cosmian Way

"I'm bored." It's a puny little phrase, yet it has the power to fill parents with a cascade of dread, annoyance, and guilt.

Thus begins The New York Times Sunday Review (February 3, 2019) Opinion Column article "Let Children Get Bored Again" by Pamela Paul, the editor of The Book Review and a co-author of the forthcoming book How to Raise a Reader. "Boredom spawns creativity and self-sufficiency," she argues.

The Artist's Way by Julia Cameron has sold more than four million copies, as the author puts it "that has been a lodestar for blocked writers and other artistic hopefuls for more than a quarter of a century."

The first printing was about 9,000 copies, said Joel Fotinos, formerly the publisher at Tarcher/Penguin, which published the book. According to Mr. Fotinos, there was concern that it wouldn't sell. "Part of the reason," Mr. Fotinos said, "was that this was a book that wasn't like anything else. We didn't know where to put it on the shelves—did it go in religion or self-help? Eventually, there was a category called "creativity," and "The Artist's Way" launched it."

Now an editorial director at St. Martin's Press, Mr. Fotinos said he is deluged with pitches from authors claiming they've written "the new Artist's Way." "But for Julia, creativity was a tool for survival," he said. "It was literally her medicine and that's why the book is authentic, and resonates with many people."

Needless to say, this must be the case for everybody, young and old, not just for writers and so-called "artists." Each and every one of us was born with "creativity" in order to swim, not to sink.

Just as Kahlil Gibran (1883-1931) comments in his book of aphorisms, poems, and parables, Sand and Foam (1926):

I am forever walking upon these shores,
Betwixt the sand and the foam.
The high tide will erase my footprints,
And the wind will blow away the foam.
But the sea and the shore will remain
Forever.

Once I filled my hand with mist.
Then I opened it and lo, the mist was a worm.
And I closed and opened my hand again, and behold there was a bird.
And again I closed and opened my hand, and in its hollow stood a man with a sad face, turned upward.
And again I closed my hand, and when I opened it there was naught but mist.
But I heard a song of exceeding sweetness.

You may have heard of the Blessed Mountain.
It is the highest mountain in our world.
Should you reach the summit you would have only one desire, and that to descend and be with those who dwell in the deepest valley.
That is why it is called the Blessed Mountain.

Every thought I have imprisoned in expression I must free by my deeds.

This is rather The Cosmian Way, methinks.

45. Great or Crazy?

In English, an iconoclast means (sacred) image-breaker. We may look at people, especially great ones, with such an iconoclastic eye. But let's look at some, whom we are told to worship, with the eye of the fictional child in *The Emperor's New Clothes*, a short tale written by Danish author Hans Christian Andersen, or *The Little Prince*, a novella, the most famous work of French writer, poet, and pioneering aviator Antoine de Saint-Exupéry, voted the best book of the 20th century (it should be, in all centuries and not only) in France (but in the whole world), for a totally different perspective.

In 1862 at the age of 34, Tolstoy proposed to the 18-year-old Sophia. Although he inherited a huge farmland with hundreds of serfs, he squandered most of his inheritance. Too busy gambling to go to a dentist, he lost most of his teeth.

Just before their wedding, he insisted that his bride read his diary about his sex life with prostitutes and serfs and even with some friends of his mother-in-law-to-be, arguing that there shouldn't be any secret between husband and wife, and that therefore they should read each other's diaries.

And consequently, there were frictions between them; still, Tolstoy went on to become a world-famous writer while Sophia gave birth to 13 children and hand-wrote all his manuscripts.

From around 1877, Tolstoy became a vegetarian, claiming that he was strictly following the teachings of Jesus. Thereafter, captivated by his "false" disciple Vladimir Chertkov, Tolstoy left home and died from pneumonia, aged 82, at the railway station of Astapovo, a remote Russian village.

It's no wonder, then, if his great love for the whole humanity didn't reach his wife and children. Would this be a case of Tolstoy alone? Didn't Buddha and Jesus leave their family homes, too? Wasn't it a bit like that with Socrates? Aren't there even today people who abandon their families and their own lives for irrational ideologies or in the name of Allah/God? Aren't there so many artists becoming alcoholics or drug addicts? What's the point, one has to wonder? Isn't it?

Let's muse over this verse written by Mahadev Desai, Mahatma Gandhi's personal secretary;

- To live with saints in heaven
- Is a bliss and a glory
- But to live with a saint on earth
- Is a different story

How on earth could one really and truly love anyone or anything, in the world before one does love oneself, first, as a Cosmian, that is, the very microcosmos of the macrocosmos, the Cosmos itself?

46. "Much Ado About Nothing"

There was a controversial news story in South Korea recently. It was about a female teacher having had a sexual relationship with a male student of hers.

It was "The world is going to the dogs," the end of the world in doomsday scenarios of "holier than thouism." Was the hysterical response of the media simply typically titillating sensationalism?

If there is no absolute truth in the world, since no human being is absolute or perfect, then we'll have to say that everything is relative. Isn't this the natural order of things, like day and night, yin and yang?

Men and women exist for each other. The sexual relationship, even though the system of traditional, sanctified, and legalized marriage changed from time to time, place to place, taking different forms of monogamy, polygamy or extramarital affairs. Didn't the marriage system itself originate from the ownership of chattels personal as items of private property?

Throughout human history, regardless of the east or the west, aren't most, if not all, sexual relationships conducted in the name of "love," dealings of either "retail" or "wholesale" trade, not to mention the porno and prostitution industry?

Let's consider the current #MeToo movement for a moment.

Anytime, anywhere, not only in the natural world but also in human societies, the bottom line is the "survival of the fittest," usually ruled by the "law of the jungle," or trade-off of goods and services between concerned and interested parties as a quid pro quo, give and take. Isn't it?

If so, is it "normal" and "as usual" for the "holy men of God" to practice sexual abuse of children and nuns, or for male teachers to have sexual relationships with their female students, whereas it's "the end of civilization" if someone like Emmanuel Macron, the present President of France (at the age of fifteen) falls in love with his 24-year-older teacher, a mother of three children including a classmate of his, and gets her divorced and marries her?

Of course, the trinity of life, love, and sex is most desirable. If, however, that is not a viable option, then, one has to enjoy them separately for convenience's sake, as the saying goes: If you do it, it's adultery; if I do it, it's a romance.

Women are said to be born with the Mother Nature, thereby, I am told that in Japan some mothers engage in sex with their teenage sons to relieve them of their sexual stress and tension, especially when they are under pressure for college entrance exams. Some years ago, when I was living in England, I read in the newspaper that in some Spanish schools they had "masturbation classes" in order to prevent teenage pregnancy and sexually transmitted disease (STD)/ venereal disease (VD) from spreading.

If sex is nothing "dirty" and love is all "sacred," both being most blissful, why not have them as much and as long as one can? As far as both are concerned, giving and taking is one and the same. Isn't it?

No wonder in Korean, we don't just say "to take." Instead, we say "to give by taking." Doesn't it make all the sense? To those who are dying to give, to be able to give all you can is the ultimate goal; whereas for those who are willing to receive what's being offered, taking what's given is your greater gift to the giver.

If you abhor and detest, as I do, the male biology of violence and war-making and admire and worship the female chemistry of love and peace-making, let's hope for the end of mankind and the advent of the womankind era back to the matriarchy. To expedite this change, I'd like to make a proposition to all women to start emulating the female praying mantises and the black widow spiders.

Anyway, in the end, both haha and hehe would make me very, very happy, indeed.

47. *An Ode to Us All*

Dear All,

Candidates for the second [2020] Annual Cosmian Prize of Nonfiction Narrative are being cordially invited to represent "Cosmian" as the Spirit of this Age (Zeitgeist).

Faced with the dire climate change resulting in the pollution of what we breathe, drink and eat, all caused by our capitalist materialism and industrial technology, we have to change our perspective and vision completely, if we are to survive as a species.

First of all, we have to realize our true identity as brief sojourners on this most beautiful and wonderful planet earth, a tiny starlet, like a leaf-boat floating in the sea of cosmos.

As such, we have to appreciate everything, including ourselves, with love and respect, believing in the oneness of us all, not only human beings and our fellow creatures but also all things in nature.

In order to come to this realization, we must get rid of all the arbitrary and self-righteous dogmatism of ideology, nationalism, racism, sexism, and whatnot; in other words, the false dichotomy between black and white, right and wrong, us and them, etc.

If I were to put 83 odd years of my lifelong credo in a nutshell, it could be this:

Writing is not to be written but to be lived; words are not to be spoken but to be acted upon; no matter how great works of arts and literature are, they are at best mere images and shadows of life and nature; no love, philosophy, religion, thought, truth or way can be caged, like the cloud, light, water and wind or stars.

Hence, the global online newspaper CosmianNews was launched in July 2018 to share our real-life narratives as described in the inaugural address.

All of us, born on this star called the planet earth to leave after a short stay, each living with whatever kind of love, in whatever style of life, in whatever color, shape and form, in one's own way, each can say something special for one sentence, as different from each other. And yet if we were to find one common denominator, could it not be that "we all are Cosmians?"

So on this proposition that "we all are Cosmians," I am inviting each one of you to share that sentence of yours. Each will be the song of a pearl-like life, or rather of a rainbow-like love

I'd like to dedicate the poem, **Praise Be** written by the American publisher of my book Cosmos Cantata, as the common motto for us all.

Praise be to those

who in their waning years
make others happy

Praise be to those

who find light in the darkness
and share it with others

Praise be to those

who can spread joy
through trust and tolerance

Praise be to those

who look far beyond themselves
to their place in the cosmos

For Lee Tae-Sang, November 15, 2013
Doris R. Wenzel

I sincerely trust that all of you will kindly accept this invitation.

Gratefully yours,

Lee Tae-Sang
Founder of CosmianNews

www.cosmiannews.com
March 1, 2020

* * *

An Endnote: Cosmian Way Is the Way to Seek

"Nobody knows everything about anything."

This is one of the principles of General Semantics launched in 1933 by Polish American originator Alfred Korzybski (1879-1950) with the publication of *Science and Sanity: An Introduction to Non-Aristotelian Systems and General Semantics.*

In other words: "We cannot imagine, think, say, understand, know all about anything or anyone—including ourselves."

"길 없는 길" (The Way Without A Way) is a four-volume narrative written by South Korean writer Choi In-ho (1945-2013) about the life journey of the famous Korean Buddhist Seeker 경허 (Gyunghuh 1849-1912).

The core message of this book *Cosmian Rhapsody* may be put this way: Cosmian Way is the way for us all to seek.

Afterword

What does it mean to live your life?
What does it mean to have lived your life?
For what and for whom one should live and die?
Where can one find the answer?

"The universe is not outside of you.
Look inside yourself;
everything that you want,
you already are."
— Rumi